D0363845

What Happens When We Die

The Ascent into the Empyrean – panel from an altarpiece thought to be of the Last Judgement (oil on panel), Bosch, Hieronymus (c.1450–1516)/Palazzo Ducale, Venice, Italy (Bridgeman Art Library)

What Happens When We Die

A Ground-Breaking Study into the Nature of Life and Death

Dr SAM PARNIA

With a foreword by Dr Peter Fenwick

HAY HOUSE
Australia – Canada – Hong Kong
South Africa – United Kingdom – United States

First published and distributed in the United Kingdom by
Hay House UK Ltd, Unit 62, Canalot Studios, 222 Kensal Rd, London W10 5BN.
Tel.: (44) 20 8962 1230; Fax: (44) 20 8962 1239.
www.hayhouse.co.uk

Published and distributed in the United States of America by
Hay House, Inc., PO Box 5100, Carlsbad, CA 92018-5100.
Tel.: (760) 431 7695 or (800) 654 5126; Fax: (760) 431 6948 or (800) 650 5115.
www.hayhouse.com

Published and distributed in Australia by
Hay House Australia Ltd, 18/36 Ralph St, Alexandria NSW 2015.
Tel.: 612 9669 4299; Fax: 612 9669 4144.
www.hayhouse.com.au

Published and distributed in the Republic of South Africa by
Hay House SA (Pty), Ltd, PO Box 990, Witkoppen 2068.
Tel./Fax: 2711-706 6612.
orders@psdprom.co.za

Distributed in Canada by
Raincoast, 9050 Shaughnessy St, Vancouver, BC V6P 6E5.
Tel.: (604) 323 7100; Fax: (604) 323 2600.

© Sam Parnia, 2005

Although every effort has been made to ensure that all owners of copyright material
have been acknowledged in this publication, the publisher would be glad to
acknowledge in subsequent reprints or editions any omissions brought to their attention.

The author of this book does not dispense medical advice or prescribe the use of any
technique as a form of treatment for physical or medical problems without the advice
of a physician, either directly or indirectly. The intent of the author is only to offer
information of a general nature to help you in your quest for well-being. In the event
you use any of the information in this book for yourself, which is your constitutional
right, the author and the publisher assume no responsibility for your actions.

A catalogue record for this book is available from the British Library.

ISBN 1-4019-0556-0

Printed and bound in Great Britain by TJ International Ltd, Padstow, Cornwall

Contents

This book is dedicated to my mother, Soraya,
who has patiently taught me and encouraged me
in all my endeavours throughout my life

Foreword

It requires a special kind of scientist to ask the question, what happens when we die? One thing is certain, and that is that we shall all die. But in our culture we tend to ignore the fact of our mortality and it is usually only when a close friend or family member is dying that we uneasily acknowledge our own inevitable progress towards death.

This is a subject that for thousands of years has largely been a question for philosophical debate rather than objective scientific exploration, but in recent times science has started to advance our understanding of what happens when we die, both physiologically and in terms of the human mind.

The work of Dr Raymond Moody and the publication of his book *Life after Life* in 1972 suggested that there was a set of phenomena, which he termed 'the near death experience', that might provide some clues about what we experience at the end of life. However, the difficulty with this early data on near death experiences was that although many people who had indeed been near death described them, the full potential of the near death experience was not understood by scientists, who saw it as just another mental state which could easily be explained by our current scientific understanding of brain function.

It took the foresight, understanding and sensitivity of Dr Sam Parnia to see the full potential of the near death experience and the contribution it could make to our understanding of death and dying. He also realized its significance as regards the most crucial problem now faced by neuroscience, the nature of consciousness. His profound realization was that our best understanding of death and dying could be achieved by studying only near death experiences which occurred during cardiac arrest, when the heart stops and after 11 seconds consciousness and brain electrical activity cease, so that no areas of brain function remain which could support consciousness. Even the very basic life-supporting systems are destroyed; respiration, cardiac output and brain-stem life-support reflexes are all absent – a state equivalent to clinical death. Dr Parnia saw that this state, which remains reversible for about 30 minutes, is the closest model that science can have of the dying process and provides a unique window of understanding into what we all experience at the end of life.

One of the most interesting features of the near death experience during cardiac arrest is that on recovery patients sometimes report leaving their bodies and watching the resuscitation process. Although many researchers have argued against their validity, workers have now suggested that many of these accounts accurately describe what actually happened. This anecdotal evidence suggests that during the time that brain function was absent the patient not only had experiences but was also able to remember these experiences, even in the absence of brain processes. This is a startling possibility. Dr Parnia single-handedly attempted to examine these claims in a preliminary study by hiding targets on the ceiling of the coronary care unit in hospital wards in Southampton to see whether they would be reported in out of body claims. This in itself tells us a great deal about him – not many doctors would have been courageous or determined enough to persuade their cautious and conservative medical colleagues to agree to this, and only a scientist who had a true vision for his scientific research would have attempted it.

For science, the important question is, does the near death experience occur and consciousness indeed continue when all brain functions are absent – something our current neuroscience regards as impossible – or does the near death experience occur either before or after the cardiac arrest, although it is interpreted by the experiencer as occurring during unconsciousness?

The recent findings are both startling and intriguing and may hold the key to discovering not just what happens when we die, but also the wider question of the nature of the self.

More studies like Dr Parnia's would tell us so much more about the nature of consciousness, and indeed what happens when we die, that to my mind science and scientific funding bodies should now make strenuous efforts to shine the laser beam of science onto this intriguing area so as to either validate or refute the possibility of continuity of consciousness beyond the brain and at the end of life.

My hope is that after reading this story, wonderfully told by Dr Parnia, not only will more people develop an understanding of what happens when we die, but that more scientists, philanthropists and forward-looking scientific bodies will agree to conduct and support the next stage of this research and so help to push forward one of the final frontiers of neuroscience.

Dr Peter Fenwick, BA, MB, BChir, DPM, FRCPsych
Consultant Neuropsychiatrist and Neurophysiologist
Institute of Psychiatry, London

Acknowledgements

No piece of work is ever accomplished without the help of the many people who, in the background and in different ways, make something possible, whether it be through encouragement, ideas, support or inspiration.

I certainly feel that I owe everything to the multitude of people who have helped me, from the philosopher Ostad Elahi, whose work, as recounted by his son Professor Bahram Elahi, sparked my initial interest, to all my colleagues, friends and family who have supported, encouraged and helped me with my research.

I would therefore like to start by thanking Professor Bahram Elahi, who with his unique, vast and extensive experience helped me to develop my research proposals and methodology during the research project. I would also like to thank Dr Peter Fenwick wholeheartedly for his constant support, enthusiasm, suggestions and encouragement, and for being such a good friend as well as a great colleague. It has been a true pleasure working with Peter. I also would like to thank Dr Derek Waller, who very kindly and enthusiastically supported me and the research locally in Southampton and helped with much of the work. I also owe sincere thanks to Heather Sloan, who has always been a pillar of support with a lovely warm smile, Becky Yeates, who helped enormously after she joined the team during the study, and all the hundreds of individuals who shared their experiences with me.

During my research many other medical colleagues also supported and encouraged me. I would like to take this opportunity to thank them all, particularly Professor Stephen Holgate, Dr John Heyworth, Professor Cyrus Cooper, Dr William Rosenberg, Professor Robert Peveler, Dr Mary Rogerson, Dr Diane Buchanan, Dr George Lewith, Dr Nigel Arden and Dr Keith Dawkins, as well as Professor Douglas Chamberlain. I must also thank Dr Susan Blackmore for her help and discussions as well as for references on the subject of near death experiences. Throughout the years she has been a great supporter of the study of consciousness and near death experiences.

During the study many others also helped me enormously and I would like to thank Marilyn Kaye, Kim D'Arcy and Sarah Watts at the hospital and university press offices as well as the drug information unit and all the staff in the hospital mail room who very kindly and enthusiastically helped with all the letters, also Debbie Kingston for her wonderful help with all my correspondence.

I would also like to thank all the resuscitation and nursing staff, especially those who worked on the medical, emergency and coronary care units throughout this study and whom I unfortunately cannot name, as the list would occupy the whole book, but without whose help this project would not have been possible.

My deepest gratitude must also go to Dr Ebby Elahi for very kindly reviewing the contents of the book, despite a very busy schedule, and for making wonderful suggestions for improvement, also Robert Kirby, my literary agent, as well as Michelle Pilley and Lizzie Hutchins, my editors at Hay House, without whose help and encouragement I could not have completed this book.

Finally, I would like to thank my wife, Lisa, my close friends and family for their support during the writing process.

Introduction

Scientific mysteries sometimes take centuries to solve. Solving them is like putting together a very complicated jigsaw puzzle. Initially it seems a haphazard mess, but you look for clues, lay a few pieces, and then, as a picture starts to form, lay more pieces until the complete picture appears. In science, the final picture can be revealed through the contribution of many individuals who have each laid down a small piece of the puzzle.

In this age, perhaps the most fascinating unsolved scientific mystery is the puzzle of life itself, of how it begins and how it ends. Although some of the mysteries surrounding the beginning of life have been explored, what happens at the end still remains an enigma. Yet this is one of the few subjects being explored by science today that is relevant to us all.

As I sit here comfortably writing this book, I am aware that with every passing second somebody somewhere in the world is faced with the question of what happens at the end of life, perhaps through simple curiosity, the loss of a loved one, news of a terminal illness or maybe even a close personal brush with death.

Very recently my wife Lisa and I were going on holiday and were driving to our hotel. We had just turned off the main road and were chatting and enjoying the warm summer afternoon. Traffic was moving steadily when suddenly the car in front stopped sharply. I was sure that Lisa had noticed this, but she seemed slow to react, so I nudged her to stop. She tried to brake, but the brakes failed. As we sped towards the stationary vehicle, I just pushed myself back into the seat, put my arm across Lisa and waited for our fate. I had no control over what was about to happen and knew that in a split-second we could be seriously hurt, or even dead.

We smashed into the car in front at speed – and then there was silence. I opened my eyes and looked across at Lisa. She appeared well. I moved my arms and legs. They were all fine. I called to Lisa, 'Are you all right?' 'Yes,' she replied. She was visibly shaken but otherwise okay. So were the passengers in the other vehicle. In fact the only ones damaged were the cars!

Later that evening, once we were over the shock, I sat and thought about what had happened. What if the brakes had failed half an hour earlier when we had been on the main road, driving at greater speed? Surely we would not have been so lucky. It had all taken place so quickly, in just a few seconds. The border between life and death had been just an instant. Thankfully we had been on the right side on this occasion, but I was all too aware that death can come to any of us at any time, without warning.

My own interest in understanding what happens at the end of life began a long time before our accident. In fact it started almost ten years earlier, when I was studying medicine in London. Training as a doctor provided me with the unique opportunity not only to learn the science of medicine but also to share many of the most intimate moments in people's lives. The insights I gained taught me so much about life itself.

I clearly remember the first time I witnessed life at the beginning. I was in the delivery suite of St Thomas' Hospital in London, assisting the birth of a young woman's baby. After hours of pain, tension and sweat, suddenly a tiny head emerged and a small baby slid out of his mother's womb. For a split-second the minuscule body was blue and lifeless and then suddenly it took its first breath, turned pink and started screaming, as if to say, 'Well, here I am!' There it was, the beginning of life, and the beginning of consciousness too, that unique sense of self-awareness and thought that accompanies us all throughout our lives. As I watched, I wondered how this had come about. How had a single cell in its mother's womb transformed into a conscious being with its own thoughts and emotions?

No one really knows exactly when consciousness begins, or what it is that makes each of us so unique. During my years as a medical student I became fascinated by these questions. I knew that the simple answer was essentially our thoughts. But I wanted to know the answer to a far more difficult question, namely how do our thoughts actually come to exist in the first place? And I soon found that the answer was not so readily available. In fact I realized that the nature of the mind was a truly undiscovered area of science, one that many consider to be the final completely untravelled frontier of the biological sciences.

During the clinical years of medical training, like most medical students I began to deal with dying patients and I soon discovered that the issue of life and death confronts most doctors on an almost daily basis. Yet what happens to the mind during the dying process still remains largely a philosophical concern rather than a medical one. I came to realize that we know very little about death, and what we do know tends to be based more on personal opinion than verifiable reality.

Perhaps the most profound event that went on to shape my thoughts and to lead me to study the nature of consciousness at the end of life was witnessing the passing away of a man called Desmond Smith in New York. Desmond was a tall, thin man of West Indian origin with a distinct Harlem accent. He lived on the outskirts of New York with his family. He had recently had his 62nd birthday. He was bright, bubbly and charming. On his birthday his family had organized a surprise party for him. One morning, Desmond began his day with what had become an inevitable bout of early morning coughing. Carrying his breakfast tray to the bedroom, he recalled his doctor's original comment: 'It's a smoker's cough.' But that day, for the first time, Desmond coughed up blood.

I was 22 and in New York as part of my final year of medical studies on a clinical attachment at Mount Sinai Hospital. It was an exciting time for me. I was at one of the finest medical institutions in the world, going through my medical adolescence into adulthood. I was attached to the pulmonary team when Desmond was rushed into Mount Sinai. My pager went off and I hurried to the emergency room, picked up the notes from the nurse and read 'Desmond Smith, hemoptysis' – a medical term for coughing up blood.

Desmond was optimistic. 'That's what I coughed up. Never mind. I'll live, doc!'

I began to examine him. There were signs of fluid surrounding the lung and I ran through a mental list of possible diseases. The most common cause of coughing up blood is a simple upper respiratory tract infection – a 'flu-like illness. But this didn't seem right in Desmond's case. Desmond was a lifelong smoker. *Perhaps lung cancer,* I thought. His vital signs were strong, so I decided to order further tests. But whatever Desmond had, it didn't seem to be a life-threatening emergency.

I left the emergency room. No more than 30 minutes later my pager went off again.

'Cardiac arrest: Emergency area. Cardiac arrest: Emergency area.'

This was real medicine, real life and death stuff. Adrenaline rushed through me. As I ran down to the emergency area, I was thinking, *What kind of emergency could this be?*

A bay had been curtained off. Nurses were rushing about. I pulled the curtains aside. A team of doctors was frantically working. One was kneeling by the man's head hurriedly trying to secure his airway. There was blood everywhere. Time sped up for me as I realized I knew this man.

'Pulse check, rhythm check …' 'VF …' 'Shock …' 'Stand clear. Oxygen away!' Thud, thud … 'Get intravenous access.' '1mg epinephrine stat.' 'Continue with CPR …' 'Start a bag of gelofusin.' 'Blood's pouring out of his mouth, he's bleeding extensively …' 'Suction, quick!' 'Get the double lumen endobronchial tube. Get the emergency bronchoscope. We've got to find the bleeding vessel …' '1mg epinephrine stat.' 'Cross match.' 'Universal blood stat.' 'Squeeze the bag of fluids …' 'Asystole … flatline … 1mg epinephrine, 3mg atropine stat …' 'Continue resuscitation.' 'I can't see anything – it's just a red sea of blood down there …' 'It's impossible to resuscitate him, he's clotted up his airways …'

Desmond was dead. He'd gone – one minute here, the next nothing. What had happened to him, to the person I had been talking to an hour ago? What was left of him? Just a lifeless body.

The interval between life and death had been so quick. Questions buzzed around my head. What had Desmond experienced? Had he been able to see us trying to resuscitate him? What had happened to him now? Could he have retained some form of consciousness or was that the end? I did not know the answers.

I stayed in New York for a few more months, but the death of Desmond had a deep impact on my life. So deep in fact that in the coming months I decided to pursue the answers to my questions through the tool I had begun to learn and could rely on the most: science.

Since then, I have spent much of my time trying to understand what happens when we die. Although I realize that traditionally this has been considered to lie in the realms of religion and philosophy, I believe that everything, including the question of what happens to us at the end of life, can be studied through the objectivity of science. Indeed, in only the last few years mainstream science has shown an interest in investigating these very issues. This is a very new area of science and may at first appear somewhat unconventional, yet I genuinely think that there is no other area of research as potentially rewarding for all of humankind.

After I started my research I found to my surprise that many more people than I had ever imagined were interested in the subject. These included people of all medical backgrounds – medical colleagues, nurses, pharmacists, physiotherapists, dieticians and many more – and from all walks of life. In fact it seemed to be a subject that drew almost universal interest. Perhaps this is because one day it will touch us all at a very personal level.

What has been discovered so far is perhaps just the tip of an iceberg, but it has huge implications for us all. It may even hold the key to the nature of human consciousness itself. Although the story is still not complete, this is a very exciting era. We are now at the point where we have both the tools and the means to answer scientifically the age-old question of what happens when we die.

1

Near Death Experiences from Antiquity to the Present Day

As a child I was always very curious about how things worked. I used to spend hours trying to 'make' things that 'worked'. To my great disappointment, they usually didn't work at all, but this didn't stop me from trying! Like most children I spent most of my time exploring the world around me and asking lots of questions – sometimes too many for my parents' liking!

Nevertheless, my parents encouraged the pursuit of learning. They also attached great importance to ethical behaviour, though they were not particularly interested in religion. I remember my father often used to deny the existence of God. He used to tell me that there was too much injustice in the world to account for God. My mother sometimes believed in God and sometimes she wasn't sure. At school I was taught basic religious education and sometimes I would go back home and tell my father what I had been taught and he would just brush it off as nonsense!

When I was about 15 or 16 years old I watched a very interesting television documentary on near death experiences, or NDEs as they are now called. This was the first time I had heard of people describing a sense of separating from their body when close to death. At that time I also came across a book describing people's experiences when close to death. What was most striking was the similarity of all the experiences – seeing a bright light, a tunnel and a heavenly place – and the many cases of people in a coma who had described being able to watch what had happened to them from above. I was fascinated by the claims that dying or unconscious people had accurately described what had happened to them and that their doctors had confirmed what they had said. Many people also seemed to believe that this indicated an afterlife. Although I was somewhat sceptical, nevertheless the accounts were very interesting ...

As I grew older, my childhood curiosity gradually became more focused on the human body and how it functioned. I remember the day I understood how cells produced proteins. It was a miracle to me how these tiny little cells accurately assembled and manufactured all the proteins that made up our body. *How wonderful the human body is,* I thought. It was this curiosity and interest in the human body, together with a sense of caring, that led me to study medicine at university.

In October 1990, I entered medical school. Like many other students I was initially shocked into a state of submission by the sheer volume of work that was needed to pass my exams, and like many others in the first term I failed some and passed some until I finally found my feet, started working hard and consistently and eventually passed my first two years. During this time, as well as living in a state of constant worry, my friends and I also had lots of fun. Our course entailed performing many experiments on one another, such as putting tubes down one another's stomachs, pouring alcohol in and watching what happened as the stomach acid levels rose. We also took blood from one another. I will never forget my friend Ali's face when he saw me approaching his arm with a needle! He pressed himself back into the seat, turned as white as a sheet and begged, '*Please* be careful – there might be a nerve behind the vein!'

One day in the lab, as I was sitting looking down a microscope at a collection of single cells and noting their structure, my thoughts drifted to another problem: *How? How can these brain cells actually give rise to thoughts?* They were cells just like any others – why should they produce thoughts? How do our thoughts arise?

As time went on, the area that I became most interested in was the brain, specifically the relationship between the mind and the brain. I was fascinated by what it was that made every one of us unique. At that time I believed very strongly that the answer to this question lay somewhere in the brain. I worked very hard during my neuroscience modules and almost took time off for a separate degree in neuroscience, except that I soon realized, to my disappointment, that this would probably not help me in my quest. The problem was that science did not yet have the answer to my questions.

The next three years of my life were spent training in clinical medicine. Here I started to deal with real patients and to face real life and death questions. During this time I observed how little we knew about the dying process and how human awareness came to exist. In my final year, meeting Desmond and watching him pass away really brought all these experiences together and raised many questions in my mind. However, on my return to England I had to focus almost solely on passing my final examinations in medicine and had no time to think of anything else.

One morning, with a few weeks left to my final exams, I was going through the monotony of studying when my mother, who knew I was interested in near death experiences, called out, 'Come and watch this on TV!' Looking for an excuse to stop studying, I decided to take a 'quick' break …

It was a programme on near death experiences. There were numerous experts talking about the subject, many of whom were presenting their own theories almost as 'facts', though they were not yet proven. I was very disappointed by this and thought it was not scientific. There was one expert, however, who drew my attention. He was Dr Peter Fenwick, a neuropsychiatrist and neurophysiologist based at King's College Hospital in London, who was widely recognized as an international authority on the mind and brain. He gave a very honest summary of the different NDE theories and conceded, 'We still do not know why near death experiences occur.' I liked his modesty and honesty, and thought, *If we don't yet know, then how are we going to find out? There must be a way to study this through science.*

A few weeks later I discussed my interest in near death experiences with my university tutor, a professor of psychiatry, who confessed that he knew very little about the subject and suggested that the best person to speak to was a fellow psychiatrist, Dr Peter Fenwick! I knew I had to try and arrange to see him – I just had to pass my exams first!

After years of studying, worrying and thinking it would never happen, finally I qualified as a doctor in the summer of 1995. I was truly ecstatic. A good friend of mine said I spent the whole summer 'almost on the clouds'!

After a break and a holiday in France, I came back to England feeling much more relaxed and ready to focus on the questions that had been on my mind ever since I had met Desmond in New York. I decided the best way to find the answers was to do the work myself. That way I would be sure of it and then I could also make the results available to others.

My first port of call was Dr Fenwick. I called up his secretary, Maureen, but she said, 'It is impossible to meet him in the next few months as he is going on a lecture tour to the Far East and is fully committed until his return. I can book you in to see him in two months' time, if that is okay?'

'*Two months?*' I said.

She must have felt sorry for me then, as she added, 'Well, come by tomorrow lunchtime and maybe he will see you between appointments – but I can't promise anything.'

At that time Dr Fenwick had just published a book on near death experiences, *The Truth in the Light*, which was a critical examination of over 300 cases selected from approximately 3,000 that had been sent to him. I was quite nervous about meeting this highly respected doctor and wanted to make a good impression, so I went out and bought the book.

King's College Hospital was in a rundown area of London and Dr Fenwick's office was at the end of an old Victorian corridor. I turned up at lunchtime and waited outside the office. Finally a tall slim man with grey hair appeared and walked towards me. As he approached, I stood up and nervously clutched his book to my chest, pushing it up a notch so that he would notice it and perhaps stop and talk to me. But instead he looked at me in a rather bemused fashion and walked straight past me to his secretary. Fortunately, she had a word with him and then he came back and was very welcoming and warm. My nervousness quickly disappeared as I relaxed and explained why I was there.

'I am sorry I don't have much time today,' he said, 'as I have a clinic until 9 p.m. tonight. Can you come back tomorrow? I have an hour free then.'

This was the beginning of a friendship that developed over the next 18 months. During this time I came to know both Peter and his wife Elizabeth and really enjoyed their company. They were very kind and gracious people with a real zest for life. We met a number of times and discussed near death experiences and the various research possibilities.

Our paths were very different. He was an eminent neuro-psychiatrist who had almost reached the end of his career, while I was starting my first job as a doctor. In the next few months he went to

Malaysia and gave lectures, while I went to Medway and learned how to put in venous catheters while trying to stay awake after sleepless nights!

One evening I went to the small hospital library and searched under 'near death experiences' on the medical database. I only got 55 or so results back – not very encouraging for a subject that had received so much media attention in the last 20 years. Any other subject and I would have found hundreds or even thousands of entries per year.

With the help of the British Library I began to search through the medical literature to find out what research had already been done on near death experiences. I soon realized that in order to study the phenomenon objectively it was important to examine a number of key questions:

1. Were these experiences a modern phenomenon or had they been a part of the dying process since ancient times?
2. How common were the experiences and were they associated with a particular personality type, culture or age?
3. How could we classify NDEs, as opposed to other mental states and experiences?
4. How could the occurrence of NDEs be explained scientifically?

Examining the medical literature, it became clear to me that these questions were in fact those that had occupied researchers in the 1970s and 1980s, and some of the answers were already available.

The First Scientific Studies

It wasn't really until as late as the mid-1970s that the study of the human mind during the dying process began to enter the realms of science. Before then it had been considered a matter for religion and philosophy only. The scientific community's interest had started when Ray Moody, an American doctor and former university lecturer in philosophy, published his bestselling book *Life After Life* in 1975. In this book Moody had collected the accounts given by 150 survivors of near death encounters. Remarkably, he found that they had all described similar experiences. These included feeling at peace, separating from their body, seeing a bright light, seeing a tunnel, seeing deceased relatives, entering a heavenly domain and having a life review. At the time these people had been unconscious. The experiences had often had a positive effect on their lives, leaving them more pious, religious and less afraid of death. Moody had termed these experiences 'near death experiences'.

At the beginning of the book Moody had provided an 'ideal' or 'complete' near death experience based upon all the common NDE features. He emphasized that this was not a particular person's experience, but rather a model or composite of the features commonly found in NDE accounts:

'A man is dying and, as he reaches the point of greatest physical distress, he hears himself pronounced dead by his doctor. He begins to hear an uncomfortable noise, a loud ringing or buzzing, and at the same time feels himself moving very rapidly through a long dark tunnel. After this, he suddenly finds himself outside of his own physical body, but still in the immediate physical environment, and he sees his own body from a distance, as though he is a spectator. He watches the resuscitation attempt from his unusual vantage point and is in a state of emotional upheaval. After a while, he collects himself and becomes more accustomed to his odd condition. He notices that he still has a "body," but one of a very different nature and with very different powers from the physical body he has left behind. Soon other things begin to happen. Others come to meet and to help him. He glimpses the spirits of relatives and friends who have already died, and a loving warm spirit of a kind he has never encountered before—a being of light—appears before him. This being asks him a question, non-verbally, to make him evaluate his life and helps him by showing him a panoramic, instantaneous playback of the major events of his life. At some point he finds himself approaching some sort of barrier or border, apparently representing the limit between earthly life and the next life. Yet he finds that he must go back to the earth, that the time for his death has not yet come. At this point he resists, for by now he is taken up with his experiences in the afterlife and does not want to return. He is overwhelmed by intense feelings of joy, love, and peace. Despite his attitude, though, he somehow reunites with his physical body and lives.

'Later he tries to tell others, but he has trouble doing so. In the first place, he can find no human words adequate to describe these unearthly episodes. He also finds that others scoff, so he stops telling other people. Still, the experience affects his life profoundly, especially his views about death and its relationship to life.' (From *Life After Life* by Ray Moody, published by Rider. Reprinted with permission of The Random House Group Ltd.)

Moody went on to observe that most of the people who had had an NDE did not experience so many of the above features. They may have only recalled a limited number of them, maybe five or six. Also the sequence in which the features took place varied – somebody may have had an out of body experience at the beginning of their NDE, for example, while another person may have seen a light at the beginning and have had an out of body experience at the end.

After the publication of *Life After Life*, NDEs became the subject of controversy and debate. While many people claimed that these experiences provided a glimpse of the afterlife, others, in particular within the scientific community, were more cautious, claiming that they were at best hallucinations and at worst fabrications.

The years that followed saw a rise in the number of reports of out of body and near death experiences. Some claimed that this was due to the recent publicity and that some of the accounts had been fabricated by attention-seekers. When researchers began to study these accounts in more detail, however, they found very little evidence to support this view, as many of the accounts pre-dated the 1970s. In fact some of the accounts went back decades, even centuries. Also, in the vast majority of cases the people involved consistently declined any publicity and were only prepared to share their experiences with researchers. Often they had not even mentioned them to their close family and friends.

Interestingly, in the 1980s reports had also started coming in of people who had experienced negative NDEs. These people often described frightful vacuums, demons, zombie-like creatures, tortures and other unpleasant experiences. It wasn't at all clear, though, whether these had really taken place when the people had been close to death or whether they had simply been due to the symptoms of a severe illness, such as excess carbon dioxide in the blood, which I knew could sometimes give rise to such negative experiences.

HISTORICAL NDEs

In the months that passed, as I examined the medical literature further, I found that there had been many accounts of near death experiences in different cultures and times. In fact the oldest reference to an NDE occurs in Plato's *Republic*, written in the fourth century BC. Here, an ordinary soldier, Er, suffers a near-fatal injury on the battlefield, is revived in the funeral parlour and describes a journey from darkness to light accompanied by guides, a moment of judgement, feelings of peace and joy, and visions of extraordinary beauty and happiness.

Although the case from Plato could have simply represented the philosophical and religious views of the afterlife prevalent at the time, I also came across a very interesting work by Hieronymus Bosch, the famous fifteenth-century Dutch painter. In a painting entitled 'Ascent into the Empyrean' he had depicted what looked like a typical NDE: a passage down a tunnel towards a bright light with people being taken there by angels (*see Frontispiece*). I wondered whether Bosch had experienced an NDE himself or whether someone else had described one to him.

Then I came across another very interesting historical case. An admiral with the British navy had narrowly escaped drowning in Portsmouth harbour in 1795. Following his ordeal he had described his experience in a local newspaper:

'Though the senses were ... deadened, not so the mind; its activity seemed to be invigorated in a ratio which defies all description, for thought rose above thought in rapid succession. The event just occurred ... the awkwardness producing it ... the bustle it must have occasioned ... the effect on my most affectionate father ... the moment in which it would be disclosed to the family, and a thousand other circumstances minutely associated with home were the first reflections. Then they took a wider range, our last cruise ... a former voyage and shipwreck, my school and boyish pursuits and adventures. Thus travelling backwards, every past incident of my life seemed to glance across my recollection in retrograde succession; not however in mere outline, as here stated, but the picture filled up with every minute and collateral feature. In short, the whole period of my existence seemed to be placed before me in a kind of panoramic review, and each part of it seemed to be accompanied by a consciousness of right or wrong, or by some reflection on its cause or consequences; indeed many trifling events which had been forgotten then crowded into my imagination, and with the character of recent familiarity.'

These two historical cases fascinated me. They were only anecdotes but obviously demonstrated that NDEs were definitely not just a modern phenomenon.

I then came across the first systematic and scientific study of NDEs. Albert Heim, a nineteenth-century Swiss geologist and mountaineer, had survived a near-fatal mountaineering accident and had gone on to collect 30 first-hand accounts from other survivors of near-fatal mountaineering accidents. He found that they had all had similar experiences. His own was typical:

'... no grief was felt nor was there any paralysing fright. There was no anxiety, no trace of despair or pain, but rather calm seriousness, profound acceptance and a dominant mental quickness. The relationship of events and their probable outcomes were viewed with objective clarity, no confusion entered at all. Time became greatly expanded.'

Heim found that in many cases there then followed a sudden review of the person's entire past and finally they often heard 'beautiful music' and fell into what they visualized as 'a superbly blue heaven containing roseate cloudlets'. Heim's work was published in 1892.

HOW COMMON WERE NDEs?

Looking through the literature, it became obvious that in the late 1970s and throughout the 1980s research had predominantly centred on characterizing the different features of the near death experience. In addition, researchers had wanted to find out more about the nature of the experience and how often it occurred.

The best account of the prevalence of NDEs had come from a Gallup survey carried out in the US in 1982. This survey had concluded that near death experiences had occurred in approximately 8 million people, or 4 per cent of the population. As I read this, I thought it was an astonishingly high proportion, much higher than I would have imagined. Unfortunately there hadn't been any more studies to confirm these findings and there were no data regarding the overall prevalence of the phenomenon in other countries.

Although it was obvious that further work was needed to fully understand how prevalent the near death experience was in society on the whole, nevertheless this survey indicated that it was probably quite common and certainly far more common than most people had thought.

DID RELIGION AND CULTURE AFFECT NDEs?

Some studies had been carried out with the aim of studying the NDE phenomenon in non-Western cultures. Obviously, understanding the role of culture was vital. If all the experiences reflected people's preconceived ideas, this would support the notion that NDEs were based upon individuals' own backgrounds rather than a universal phenomenon that transcended cultural and religious views.

Historically, I found that events closely resembling NDEs had been described by Bolivian, Argentinean and North American Indians and had appeared in Buddhist texts, Islamic texts and accounts from China, Siberia and Finland. The most common features were: a) having an out of body experience; b) a reunion with ancestors and departed friends; c) an experience of light accompanied by joy and peace; d) a border or dividing line between the living and the dead.

In more modern times, near death experiences had been described in many areas of the world, including India, China, South America and the Middle East. Interestingly, in these countries relatively little if any publicity had been given to the phenomenon.

In the cases recalled by people in non-Western cultures it had been found that although the central features were universally present, the interpretation of the experience may have reflected personal religious or cultural views. In other words, during a close encounter with death, people from different parts of the world may have all felt peaceful, seen a tunnel, a bright light and a being of light, and had the sensation of detaching from their bodies, but they may have identified the being of light according to their own cultural and religious backgrounds. In one study, for example, carried out in 1985, the experiences of 16 Asian Indians had been compared with those of Americans and it had been found that the Indians had often encountered Yamraj, the Hindu king of the dead, while the Americans had not.

The largest cross-cultural study had been carried out in 1977 by Osis and Haraldsson and had focused more on deathbed visions. These are the experiences that people have before death, usually in the 24 hours prior to death, and they are different from the classic near death experiences. Deathbed visions are usually reported by carers who have looked after a person during the dying process. In this study the researchers had examined the visions of approximately 440 terminally ill American and Indian patients as described to their doctors and nurses. The most common feature, which occurred in 91 per cent of cases, was seeing deceased relatives. In 140 cases there were reports of seeing religious figures, usually described as an angel or God. Where these were specifically identified, they were always described according to the person's religious beliefs: no Hindu reported seeing Jesus, and no Christian a Hindu deity.

I soon came to realize that the central features of the NDE had been recorded throughout history and across numerous cultures and religious groups. The experience had also been described by atheists as well as those with a particular faith, whether practising or non-practising. But what of personality?

DID PERSONALITY AFFECT NDEs?

In the 1980s several researchers had investigated whether there was a relationship between a particular type of personality and having an NDE. In other words, they wanted to find out whether certain people had a predisposition to having the experience.

In one study a comparison was made between people who had had an NDE and people who had not, as regards IQ levels, an extroverted personality, a neurotic personality and anxiety. No significant differences were found. In another study researchers found no difference in measures of hysterical tendencies, death anxiety, danger seeking and psychotic personality.

Other studies had suggested that there might be an increased likelihood of prior mystical experiences in those who had NDEs. This was interesting, although I wondered whether there was possibly a limitation associated with these studies in that they had involved somewhat biased samples of people. Essentially the people used in the studies had volunteered their experiences and therefore may have represented a specific group of people who were more likely to have had prior mystical experiences and therefore more likely to volunteer them to investigators. It wasn't clear whether the reason for the difference wasn't simply that people without prior mystical experiences were less likely to come forward.

DID NDEs ALSO OCCUR IN CHILDREN?

Without doubt the most interesting group of individuals to have reported NDEs were children. Some investigators and commentators had argued that adults might have imagined NDEs based upon their own personal cultural and religious views, but the children in the studies were often too young to have formed an opinion regarding the afterlife, or even death itself. I was curious to know if their experiences were the same as those of adults or different in some way.

The most research on NDE in children had been done by Dr Melvin Morse, an American paediatrician. He had looked at many critically ill children admitted to the intensive care unit and had found that some had in fact described near death experiences. These experiences had shared many of the same features as those of adults – separating from the body, watching events, feeling peaceful, seeing a bright light and beings of light – but had often been described in children's terminology and during the course of play, sometimes over many months. The children's interpretation of what they had seen had been based upon their own level of comprehension, but it was nevertheless clear that they had had similar experiences to adults. Significantly, although some of the children described by Morse had been around nine or ten years old, others had been very young, just three to five years old. This group was certainly too young to have had any real concept of death and the afterlife and it was fascinating that they had had similar experiences to adults.

In one of his published scientific articles Morse had quoted a number of the children's NDEs. An eight-year-old boy who had almost drowned after his parents' car had swerved off an icy road into a river in Washington had reported: 'I could see the car filling up with water, and it covered me all up. Then everything went blank. Suddenly I was floating in the air. I felt like I could swim in the air.' He was very surprised to still be thinking, as he knew he must have died. He continued, 'Then I floated into the huge noodle. Well, I thought it was a noodle, but maybe it was a tunnel. Yeah, it must have been a tunnel because a noodle doesn't have a rainbow in it.'

A five-year-old girl whose heart had stopped had reported: 'I rose up in the air and saw a man like Jesus because he was nice and he was talking to me. I saw dead people, grandmas and grandpas, and babies waiting to be born. I saw a light like a rainbow which told me who I was and where I should go. Jesus told me it wasn't my time to die.'

The youngest case was that of a six-month-old baby. This baby had been admitted to the intensive care unit of Massachusetts General Hospital with severe kidney failure. He had survived and been discharged home with his parents. As he was growing up his parents noticed that whenever he went through a tunnel he would have a panic attack. This happened for example if they were driving through a tunnel or when the child was playing with his siblings and went through a playground tunnel. Eventually, when he was four, his parents had attempted to explain the imminent death of his grandfather and he had said that he had died too and had related his experience in the ICU. I really wanted to know more about this experience, but the researchers had not reported it in detail.

I was intrigued by these experiences in children and really wanted to interview a child myself. Later I had the good fortune to be contacted by someone whose grandchild had had an NDE, but in the meantime I carried on trying to answer some of my own fundamental questions through the study of the medical literature. One of my questions was how we could classify NDEs as opposed to other mental states and experiences.

RESEARCH SCALES USED TO CLASSIFY NDEs

By looking at the features described by Moody and other investigators it was obvious that many of the features that made up an NDE were by no means specific to those who had come close to death. In fact there were many examples of people who were perfectly well or physically ill but not close to death having feelings of joy and peace and/or seeing a bright light. In order for the experience to be classified as an NDE there needed to be a series of common features and not just one or two. In the same way that we could not claim that anyone who felt intensely peaceful, for example, had experienced an NDE, neither could we claim that anyone who had experienced seeing a light had also had an NDE. So how might we differentiate between an NDE and other experiences? Obviously a research scale was needed. I found two that had been devised in the 1980s by two different American researchers.

The Weighted Core Experience Index

In order to allow researchers to differentiate between near death and other experiences, in 1980 Kenneth Ring, an American psychologist, devised a ten-point interview scale which allowed the experiences to be standardized and measured. He named his research scale 'the Weighted Core Experience Index'.

Ring then went on to analyse the experiences of 102 people who had come close to death. He found that based upon this weighted scale, 48 per cent of his group had experienced an NDE.

Having examined the cases, Ring concluded that there was a 'core experience' which unfolded in a characteristic pattern. The stages that he described were:

a) An experience of peace, well-being and absence of pain
b) A sense of detachment from the physical body, progressing to an out of body experience
c) Entering darkness, a tunnel experience with panoramic memory and predominantly positive effect
d) An experience of a light which is bright, warm and attractive
e) Entering the light, meeting persons or figures.

The Greyson Scale

In 1983 Bruce Greyson, a psychiatrist who is currently a professor at the University of Virginia, criticized the Ring scale as being based upon 10 arbitrary points and devised another measurement scale, which he based upon interviews with 74 people who had had NDEs. He then collected the 16 most frequently encountered features, as recalled by his sample of 74 people, and developed a 16-point questionnaire, which he termed 'the Greyson scale' (see Table 1.1).

Table 1.1 The Greyson Scale

1. Experiencing an altered state of time
2. Experiencing accelerated thought processes
3. Life review
4. Sense of sudden understanding
5. Feelings of peace
6. Feelings of joy
7. Feelings of cosmic oneness
8. Seeing/feeling surrounded by light
9. Having vivid sensations
10. Extrasensory perception
11. Experiencing visions
12. Experiencing a sense of being out of physical body
13. Experiencing a sense of an 'otherworldly' environment
14. Experiencing a sense of a mystical entity
15. Experiencing a sense of deceased/religious figures
16. Experiencing a sense of a border or point of no return

The Greyson scale gives each of the 16 features a score of 0, 1 or 2. The score depends first on whether the feature has been experienced and second on how intense the experience has been. Therefore, using this scale, anyone's experience can be graded and given a score. There is a potential maximum score of 32, but for an experience to be defined as an NDE Greyson stated that a minimum score of 7 was needed.

Since the early 1980s research studies have used one of these two scales to standardize and compare the NDE experiences recounted by people. Although both research scales have some limitations in their day-to-day applications, they have been particularly useful during research as they have provided a basic means of defining an NDE and semi-quantifying the depth of the experience. For example, one person may have a score of 8 on the Greyson scale, whereas somebody else may have a score of 16. The person with the higher score is very likely to have experienced eight to ten features of an NDE, whereas the other person has probably experienced four to six features.

Potential Future Work to Improve NDE Scales

While studying the research scales devised by Drs Ring and Greyson, I began to think that they had certain limitations and future research should focus on developing other research scales.

Both scales currently in use were either based or tested upon subjective NDE accounts given by people many years after the event. From a scientific point of view researchers were thus limited by the fact that they could not ascertain objectively how close to death an individual had really been. This was because in the majority of cases researchers did not have access to the medical records from the time of the experience and so were necessarily limited to what the patient described of their condition. In some cases this may have been sufficient to ascertain that the patient's life was in danger, as they may have been told by medical staff that they had suffered a cardiac arrest or other critical condition, but this was not universal. Therefore, an improved standard scale would be one based upon recalled experiences from patients who had been proven to have been medically close to death. Experiences recalled from such a period could then truly be called 'near death' or even actual 'dying' experiences.

Scientific Arguments for the Causation of NDEs

Although at first some scientists had been sceptical about whether NDEs even occurred, in modern times most researchers had come to accept that they did take place and the main area of debate had focused around their possible cause and significance. I found that three broad views had been proposed to account for the causation of NDEs.

BRAIN-BASED THEORIES: HALLUCINATIONS

The most widely accepted scientific arguments had largely centred around the concept that the experience was a hallucination in response to changes in the brain at the time of death. It had been argued that although NDEs might seem real to those who had experienced them, there were nevertheless physiological and chemical derangements accompanying the process of death which might as a consequence also cause hallucinations. These chemical changes were thought to cause the near death experience. It was also well known that hallucinations often seemed very real to the person experiencing them but did not correspond to objective reality.

To support this argument many brain mediators had been proposed to account for the experiences, although none had yet been shown to be responsible experimentally. These included a lack of brain oxygen, increased carbon dioxide, the release of endorphins (the body's own morphine-like substance), a specific type of seizure known as temporal lobe epilepsy, various drugs and in particular drugs that were known to cause hallucinations, such as ketamine (which is occasionally used as an anaesthetic).

The 'Dying Brain' Hypothesis

THE ROLE OF OXYGEN

The basic brain-based theory as proposed by Dr Blackmore, a well-known psychologist and NDE researcher from Bristol, has become known as the 'dying brain' hypothesis. This theory proposed that different events such as severe stress, extreme fear and a lack of brain oxygen, which can all occur during the dying process, may cause uncontrolled activity in the brain areas responsible for vision and thus lead to the illusion of seeing a light and tunnel.

This was quite an elegant theory and was based upon how the cells in the brain worked. In daily life the vast majority of our vision comes from the middle part of our field of vision, with relatively very little coming from the outer fields or peripheral fields (central vision versus peripheral vision). This is why we have to use our central vision for all activities that require concentration, such as reading. The brain and the eye therefore have many cells devoted to analysing information from the central portion of vision and relatively few cells devoted to analysing information from the peripheral portion of vision. Dr Blackmore suggested that lack of oxygen to the brain may activate cells in the back of the brain and as there are more cells involved in central vision, this may in turn create the illusion of seeing a bright light in the middle. As there are also fewer cells involved in peripheral vision, there may be relatively less activation of those cells, creating the impression of a bright light in the centre that fades out towards the periphery, or in other words, a tunnel effect.

Support for this theory came from reports by certain high-speed fighter pilots. Due to the tremendous speeds reached by Air Force jets, any sudden change in direction places an incredibly high pressure (G force) on the body of the pilot, which can lead to a sudden reduction in the flow of blood to the brain. This could cause a pilot to lose consciousness in mid-flight, with potentially fatal consequences. When experiencing this 'G-LOC' phenomenon, some pilots had reported dream-like states, as well as feelings of detachment and euphoria. Since these experiences had some similarities to some of the features of NDE and occurred as a consequence of a lack of oxygen to the brain, some scientists had argued that perhaps NDEs also occurred as a consequence of a lack of oxygen to the brain.

The G-LOC was an interesting phenomenon because when someone is dying it is typical that there is reduced flow of blood to the brain. This is what the high-speed jets were inducing artificially in the pilots, so maybe the body really thought it was about to die. This could potentially account for the similarities with NDEs, although there had not been any reports of an actual NDE during G-LOC.

Although I thought this lack of oxygen theory was very well thought out, I could see a number of areas where it didn't fit with the observations regarding NDEs and with medical practice. First, many people had reported having an NDE just before a moment of life-threatening danger, for example just before the impact of a car accident. These people could not have had lower than normal oxygen levels, as they had been physically untouched at the moment when they had had the NDE. Furthermore, others had reported having an NDE even when they had not been critically ill and so would have had normal oxygen levels.

From a medical point of view, lack of oxygen is a very common problem in hospital. Most doctors working with emergencies come across it regularly, particularly in patients whose lungs or hearts are not working very well, for example in cases of severe asthma or heart failure. I had looked after probably more than 100 patients with a lack of oxygen. When oxygen levels fall, patients become agitated and acutely confused. This 'acute confusional state', as it is known medically, is very different from the near death experience. During it people develop 'clouding of consciousness' together with highly confused thought processes with little or no memory recall. Unlike NDEs, which are typically universal well-structured thought pro-cesses with reasoning and memory formation, such experiences are fragmented and not universal. Also, those who have NDEs have an excellent memory of the experience, which often stays with them for decades. This is the complete opposite of an acute confusional state.

If the dying brain theory were correct, then I would expect that as the oxygen levels in patients' blood dropped, they would gradually develop the illusion of seeing a tunnel and/or a light. In practice, patients with low oxygen levels do not report seeing a light, a tunnel or any of the typical features of an NDE and in fact this experience has never been reported by any other doctor or scientific study as a feature of lack of oxygen.

Interestingly also, although Dr Blackmore's theory suggested a mechanism to get a bright central light that faded at the periphery, thus giving rise to the illusion of a tunnel, in reality those who described the tunnel and light never described them in that fashion. Typically they were described as a bright light that was not fading at the periphery, with a distinct tunnel which was sometimes seen as other shapes such as kaleidoscopes, etc.

THE ROLE OF CARBON DIOXIDE

When people stop breathing adequately, as the oxygen levels go down, there is also an increase in the carbon dioxide levels in the body. This is simply because there is reduced ventilation as the lungs stop working. Some scientists had proposed that NDEs might be taking place as a response to increased carbon dioxide.

In support of this some had proposed the work of an American psychiatrist, L. J. Meduna, who had treated some people with carbon dioxide in the 1950s. Some of his patients had then experienced dream-like states that had seemed very real to them.

Although this was very interesting to me, I knew that although raised carbon dioxide was an extremely common problem in clinical practice, we hardly ever saw anyone have an NDE-type event. Also, there had been many studies in the years since Meduna's work on the effects of increased carbon dioxide and these had not shown that it led to NDE-like states.

THE ROLE OF DRUGS

Scientists had also suggested that perhaps drugs administered at the time of death were causing NDEs. Examining the literature, this seemed doubtful, however, as studies had shown that NDEs associated with medication tended to be less complex than those without medication. Also, there had been many reports of people who had experienced an NDE without any medication. There were many cases, for example, of people who had had an NDE just before an accident such as falling off the side of a mountain or being involved in a car crash.

THE ROLE OF THE BRAIN CHEMICALS AND RECEPTORS
Some scientists had hypothesized about areas within the brain that might be mediating the near death experience. It is well known that certain drugs, including amphetamines, ketamine and phencyclidine (LSD), can lead to quite complex hallucinations. The way in which these drugs work is by attaching to certain receptors found in the brain, which then activates the receptors and mediates their effects. For example, ketamine and phencyclidine attach to a receptor called N-methyl-D-aspartate (NMDA), and when this is activated, complex hallucinations can result.

Dr Jansen, a doctor who specialized in the effects of drugs, had studied the effects of ketamine and had suggested that although it wasn't causing NDEs, they might be occurring due to the activation of the same areas of the brain that ketamine activated. He argued that when there is a lack of oxygen to the brain, the brain responds by releasing certain chemicals to protect itself. These chemicals can also activate the NMDA receptor. Therefore certain features of a near death experience, such as seeing a tunnel or a light, might be arising as a consequence of overactivity of this receptor in the same way that overactivity of the receptor in response to certain drugs could cause hallucinations.

This was a very well-thought-out theory that had unfortunately not been tested. It had a limitation in that the NMDA receptor is very widely found in the brain and is involved in many other activities at many other times without causing hallucinations. So it would not be sufficient to assume that its activity caused hallucinations or NDEs all the time, as in that case most of us would have hallucinations or NDEs most of the time! Also, NDEs really aren't like the hallucinations described by people who take drugs. Some scientists had therefore looked at other mechanisms.

When the body undergoes a major physical stress such as a serious illness, it releases morphine-like substances called endorphins. These can produce a sensation of well-being, happiness and peace. It had been suggested by some researchers that the peaceful feelings occurring during NDEs might be a response to the release of endorphins. Other researchers had proposed that the intermediary for this process was another brain molecule (neurotransmitter) called serotonin, which can also lead to sensations of well-being.

It made a lot of sense to suggest that endorphins caused the peaceful sensations, although again no one had tested this out in people with NDE.

NDE as a Type of Seizure: The Role of Temporal Lobe Epilepsy

Another view had been that the complex visions that took place during NDEs might have occurred due to activity in specific areas of the brain called the temporal lobes. In particular NDE had been linked with a condition called temporal lobe epilepsy. The reason why this theory had been put forward was that activity in these areas of the brain had been shown to lead to complex hallucinations. I therefore set out to study this condition in detail.

I knew that what happened during an epileptic seizure was that there was abnormal electrical activity in a specific section of the brain which led to specific changes in the rest of the body. For example, if there were increased electrical activity in the areas of the brain responsible for arm and leg movements, there would be a resultant jerking of the arms and legs, which is often what people associate with epileptic seizures. If, however, there were an abnormal change in the electrical activity of the visual areas of the brain, then people might see flashes of light or other visual images. That was why it was possible to have hallucinations during certain types of epilepsy, including temporal lobe epilepsy.

As I studied temporal lobe epilepsy, I became fascinated, although I couldn't see an obvious resemblance to NDEs. Temporal lobe epilepsy is associated with a number of specific features, which include a distorted perception of events, complex hallucinations involving sounds and visions, *déjà vu* experiences and an abnormal aura starting in the stomach, which rises up the chest and can lead to panic attacks. If a seizure is prolonged, there can also be loss of consciousness. There had also been descriptions of patients being in 'a state of unreality' and sometimes performing uncontrollable repetitive movements, or automatisms, such as chewing uncontrollably, continuously grimacing and even in some cases automatically undressing without being aware of what they were doing or remembering it afterwards.

The fact that some people with temporal lobe epilepsy had described hallucinations which appeared to share some of the features of an NDE had led some researchers to propose that NDEs were also a consequence of abnormal function in this area of the brain. I didn't see enough evidence for this. If NDEs occurred as a consequence of overactivity in the temporal and limbic areas of the brain, due for example to a lack of oxygen, one would also expect to see some of the other features of overactivity of the temporal and limbic areas, such as loss of memory, automatisms and *déjà vu* experiences. Such features did not occur in association with NDEs and when I examined the original scientific studies on overactivity of these areas of the brain I noted that NDE-like features had not been commonly described.

Although I could see that the brain-based theories discussed in the scientific literature had been developed rationally and eloquently, as they stood they did not seem sufficient to account for the NDE phenomenon. I had no doubt that the brain *was* involved with the near death experience, but there had to be other explanations. I turned to look at the other theories.

PSYCHOLOGICAL THEORIES

The second major mechanism that had been put forward to account for NDEs was a psychological one. It had been suggested that although the experience could appear very real, it had actually been constructed in the mind, either consciously or subconsciously, in response to the stress of an encounter with death (or perceived encounter with death), and did not correspond to a real event. In a way, it was similar to wish-fulfilment – because someone thought they were about to die, they experienced certain things in accordance with what they expected or wanted to occur. Imagining a heavenly place was in effect a way for them to soothe themselves through the stress of knowing that they were close to death. It had thus been proposed that the near death experience could be a form of depersonalization or dissociation.

Depersonalization is the process by which some people react to a frightening event. When this happens, people can abandon all sense of their own identity and completely separate themselves from the frightening perception. They form a fantasy and replace the terrifying experience with a pleasurable dream-like scenario that is more bearable.

Dissociation is a form of withdrawal to protect an individual from a stressful event. Under extreme circumstances some people may detach from certain unwanted feelings in order to avoid experiencing their emotional impact. One trigger for such a sensation could be a situation that may appear potentially fatal. According to this theory, NDEs could be an unconscious defence mechanism in which an individual separates themselves from specific activities or emotions in order to avoid their reality.

The main argument in support of the psychological theories was that many people who had had a close encounter with death, such as those involved in near-fatal accidents, had described experiencing many of the features of an NDE just prior to the accident. This had been a feature of the cases described by Albert Heim, the nineteenth-century geologist who had collected over 30 cases of mountaineers who had been involved in near-fatal accidents.

Furthermore, two medical researchers in the 1970s, Noyes and Kletti, had collected the NDE experiences of 104 people who had come close to death through extreme danger such as mountaineering falls and car accidents and they too had found that many of the experiences had occurred just prior to the accident.

Further evidence had come from a scientific study that had been carried out by Dr Owens and colleagues and published in the medical journal *The Lancet* in 1990. In this study the researchers had collected the medical records of people who had described an NDE and found that not all of them had been critically ill during their hospital stay.

The 'psychological comfort' theory proposed including not just the heavenly component of the near death experience, such as seeing a bright light and entering a new domain, but also the resuscitation attempts that some people had claimed to have been able to watch while supposedly out of body. It had been suggested that the brain might simply be constructing that experience from previously stored memories. Most people are now quite familiar with what happens in hospitals through the many medical programmes on television. Also, although the person might have appeared unconscious to the doctors and nurses, it has been suggested that they might have been only partly unconscious and therefore still able to gather information through their ordinary senses such as hearing. Patients who have been inadequately anaesthetized have sometimes reported being aware of events that have occurred during surgical operations as well as being able to hear conversations between the medical staff. The difference between these and out of body experiences is that these patients have simply not had adequate anaesthesia, which is very different from people in a deep coma or even with no brain function reporting being able to 'see' things that have subsequently been verified by medical and nursing staff. Nevertheless this seemed to be an interesting theory. However, it had also not been tested.

One last untested psychological theory that I came across, which also struck me as interesting, was that an NDE could be a form of reliving the trauma of birth. A baby travels from the darkness of the womb to light and is greeted by the love and warmth of the nursing and medical staff, and so, it was proposed, the dying brain could be recreating the passage through a tunnel to light, warmth and affection.

TRANSCENDENTAL THEORIES

The third viewpoint which had been expressed in the scientific literature had been by far the most controversial. It had been suggested that an NDE might be a spiritual experience indicating the existence of a soul and providing a glimpse into the afterlife, as had in fact been claimed by the vast majority of those who had experienced it.

The experts arguing this had based their case upon a number of points. First, because the experience occurred universally and had been described all over the world, they argued it was unlikely to be a hallucination. If it were, people of different cultures would be expected to have different experiences, as their memories would be dependent on their previous life experiences. Another argument against NDEs being purely psychological or hallucinatory experiences was that they had also been described by children too young to have any concept of death or an afterlife. The final argument put forward was that people experiencing an NDE had anecdotally reported being able to see things in places and at distances that they could not have known about. Dr Morse had described such accounts in children and there had also been a famous case of a lady in Seattle who had reported being out of body when critically ill and had amongst other things accurately described seeing a tennis shoe on a window ledge.

Although this spiritual view had been proposed by scientists, it had not been popular with the scientific community. Many scientists, such as Dr Blackmore, who had studied NDEs for many years, had argued against it, claiming that there was a lack of clear independent corroboration in such cases.

THE NEED FOR FURTHER RESEARCH

At the end of my search through the scientific literature I had come to understand near death experiences in much more detail. It had become clear to me that we really could not dismiss them as simple fabrications. The fact that they had been described by so many people in so many different cultures and eras went against this. It was also remarkable that right across different times, cultures and age groups people coming close to death had reported a consistent set of experiences. This suggested very strongly that at the very least NDEs offered a glimpse of what we would all experience at the end of our lives.

Unfortunately, one of the most disappointing aspects of near death experiences had been that despite the great interest by the public and the media in the 20 years since they had first been described, relatively little scientific research had been done on them. This lack of research probably reflected both the obvious difficulties encountered in objectively studying people's experiences during the dying process and to some extent an underlying prejudice within the scientific and medical communities regarding the subject. A consequence of this lack of research had been that the true significance of the phenomenon had not been fully elucidated. This had meant that 'experts' on the subject had usually expressed their underlying philosophical views rather than the findings of objective science.

The scientists whose research I had studied had laid down the first few pieces of the jigsaw puzzle of the human mind at the end of life, but I could see that so much more research needed to be done. None of the main theories had yet been tested scientifically and a major new approach was needed. I wanted to help solve this greatest of mysteries.

2

Setting up the Southampton Study

Finally, the day I had been waiting for arrived. I woke up early, dressed casually and stood gazing out of the window across the almost derelict hospital car park. It was a Saturday morning and not many people were working that day. My mind was busy. *Could it possibly work? Would it all happen as planned?* I really hoped so. I truly did.

It was a warm August morning in 1997. I drove to the small local hotel, Hotel Nirvana, to pick up Tony. Tony was a freelance film producer who used to work for the BBC science division and had worked closely with Dr Fenwick in 1987 to produce a very good documentary on NDEs. He had travelled all the way from Sussex for this ...

For a moment I thought back to the time, not that long ago, when I had been looking for a break, an inspiring idea, a hypothesis, a workable method to move the subject of NDE research forward, and now here I was not only with an idea but actually about to start the first ever study of NDEs in Britain and the first of its kind anywhere in the world.

The break I had been looking for had come almost ten months earlier, after I had been offered a three-year postgraduate training programme in internal medicine at Southampton General Hospital.

This was a university hospital with a very good reputation. I knew that being there would provide me with the stability and time needed to conduct the research that I had wanted to do since my time in New York two years earlier.

While I had been very keen, I had also been realistic. I knew that enthusiasm alone would not be enough and from a practical point of view it would be extremely difficult to carry out a study on NDEs. There were numerous problems. First, how would I find the time for research? It was almost unheard of for people to set up their own research projects during this period of their careers. Working clinically as a senior house officer or resident really left very little time to do anything else, and any spare time I had had to be dedicated to studying for the MRCP, or board examinations in internal medicine. Also, even if I somehow found the time, how would I actually manage to persuade my bosses and senior colleagues to support a study on NDEs in their hospital? The subject generally had a negative connotation in the medical community, as doctors still associated it with 'paranormal' research. Bearing this in mind, I also had to think very carefully about the possible effects on my own career. I was a young doctor just starting out and I didn't want to tarnish my reputation before I had even started. Maybe this was why others had not attempted to study NDEs in the past. I didn't know what to do, but decided to move forward anyway.

My inspiration had come during one of my meetings with Dr Fenwick the previous autumn. One evening he said to me, 'There are two areas of research that I have been thinking of recently. The first is the study of NDEs in those who are born congenitally blind. There have been anecdotal reports of congenitally blind people who have never seen anything in their lives but during a critical illness have described separating from the body and being able to see things for the first time ever! They have reported being able to recognize colours and images that they had only heard of before.'

I thought this was fascinating, but it was Dr Fenwick's second idea that really intrigued me. He went on to say, 'The other area that we could investigate could be the use of hidden targets to determine whether the people who claimed to be out of body really had been able to see things from the ceiling.'

Looking very perplexed, I said, 'How could we do that?'

'You place things around the hospital rooms or operating rooms so that they are not visible from ground level but only visible when viewed from above, say, for example, from the ceiling.'

Looking even more perplexed, I said, 'Well, how can you do that? Whatever you put in the room would be visible from ground level as well, so how would you ensure that it was only seen from the ceiling?'

Dr Fenwick leaned forward, picked up a large white envelope from his desk and said, 'Like this.'

He then drew lines and shapes on one side of the envelope, stood up and lifted the envelope above his head, so that the side with the lines and figures faced upwards towards the ceiling and the side that was clear faced downwards.

'If you look from below, what do you see?'

'Just a white envelope,' I said.

'Exactly, and if you could look from above, what would you see?

'The lines!' I said excitedly.

'Exactly – you can't see them from below, but you can from above. We need to have targets such as this in the operating rooms so that they are only visible if someone is at the level of the ceiling. Then we can test the claims of those who say they have watched doctors and nurses working from above.'

This idea seemed so simple yet so brilliant! I was thrilled! Sometimes the simplest ideas really were the best! This was truly what was needed. There had been so much debate regarding this aspect of NDEs in the literature and in the press that it really warranted a study. After all, it was the only aspect that was amenable to objective testing. All the others, such as seeing deceased relatives or a tunnel and light and entering a heavenly domain, were really personal, but the out of body component was the part where people described what others had said and done, and so it could be tested and verified.

All we had to do was get a large enough group of subjects, say for example 100 or 200 people, who claimed to have been at the ceiling looking down at the doctors and nurses while near death. If none of them could identify the images, then this would suggest that they must have imagined being up there. In this case we would have to conclude that perhaps the near death experience was simply a trick of the mind, maybe just an illusion or a hallucination. If, on the other hand, 100–200 people all identified the images without themselves or anyone else knowing about them beforehand, then we would have to accept their claims!

This would of course pose a huge problem for us scientifically, as our science simply could not account for it. Nevertheless we had to be open-minded to claims that challenged our scientific beliefs and assumptions. The NDE evidence was anecdotal, but many other areas of research had originally started off with anecdotal evidence and then progressed to great discoveries. In the case of NDEs there was now a lot of evidence that could no longer be ignored and we had to let the questions be answered by the objectivity of science, not our own personal opinions. After all, we didn't know what happened to the mind at the end of life – for that matter we didn't even know the nature of the mind. In effect by performing the study we would be testing the nature of human consciousness and its relationship with the brain at the point of death. This was really what had intrigued me ever since I had met Desmond. I was even more excited when I realized we would be the first ever group of researchers to test the theories for the causation of this phenomenon scientifically.

'That is the study that I would like to do,' I enthused. 'The study of NDEs in the blind is also very interesting, but this is the one that

I think will really help us move the whole subject forward. Nothing like this has ever been attempted before, as far as I can see.'

We agreed to move forward with this idea and I left that meeting very excited indeed.

Although the concept was truly novel, it wasn't enough on its own. We needed to test all of the three main theories proposed for the causation of NDEs. No one had ever done so before. I really wanted to test the 'dying brain' theory by examining whether lack of oxygen, increased carbon dioxide or drugs given during hospital stay cause NDEs. I also realized that we needed to test the psychological theories by examining the effects of the individuals' cultural and religious backgrounds. Finally we had to test the theory that an NDE was a transcendental event by exploring whether people claiming to be able to see events from the ceiling had really been able to do so. This idea was not compatible with mainstream scientific views and also went against what I had been taught about the mind and the brain, so I felt sceptical at times, but I realized we would only ever know if we tested the theory objectively using the hidden targets that Dr Fenwick and I had discussed.

Now the only question that remained was how to define being 'near death'. One of the main difficulties and drawbacks with NDE research so far had been that it had been almost impossible to ascertain objectively and medically how close to death people had been. This was a limitation in almost all the studies that I had seen.

The difficulty was that in all the studies the reported NDEs had often taken place many years earlier and due to a lack of medical records it had been impossible to see how close to death the people had really been. Even if the records had been available, it would have been extremely difficult for any researcher to go back and identify exactly when during a hospital stay many years earlier a certain individual had had an NDE. Although many of the people involved in the studies had been admitted to hospital with severe illnesses such as a heart attack, a stroke, meningitis or a severe episode of pneumonia, that didn't necessarily mean their lives had been in danger. Even being in the intensive care unit didn't necessarily mean that someone's life was in danger. So a method was needed to identify a group of people who were objectively on the brink of death. This had not been done in any of the previous studies.

So far the term 'near death' had unfortunately been used fairly loosely. In his book *Life after Life* Dr Moody had defined it as 'a clinical situation that would normally have led to the death of the individual without medical intervention'. However this was still not accurate enough, as I knew from experience that someone could have a potentially life-threatening illness, but due to medical intervention that illness would often not threaten their life. In fact it was our aim as doctors to ensure that a patient never reached a life-threatening situation by instigating early and appropriate treatment. Also, I knew very well from medical practice that many people with severe illnesses suffered hallucinations. Therefore we needed to be able to differentiate between the hallucinatory experiences that were taking place during severe illnesses that were not life-threatening and the experiences taking place at the point of death.

In order to overcome this obvious difficulty it was essential to study the experiences that had occurred during an objective period of clinical death. For this we needed a model of the dying process that would mimic the same biological events that take place in the body when an individual is actually dying. In clinical practice death is normally diagnosed when the heart stops beating, the person stops breathing and the brain stem (the area of the brain that is responsible for maintaining life) and hence the rest of the brain stop functioning. The ideal model was therefore one in which all these criteria were met, namely a cardiac arrest.

This was a good model for a number of reasons. First, in this condition patients develop two out of the three criteria of clinical death – no heartbeat, no breathing – and also develop the third – fixed dilated pupils of the eyes[1] – within a few seconds due to the loss of brain (and in particular brain stem) function. Secondly, it mimics the initial period of the dying process biologically. Finally, irrespective of the cause of death, the last steps in the dying process are for the person to stop breathing and the heart to stop beating – in other words a cardiac arrest. Therefore the mechanism by which everyone dies is a cardiac arrest and consequently what people experience at that time can provide us with a unique understanding of the experiences that we will all have as we die.

Some scientists, however, had argued that NDEs could not really be considered experiences of dying, as obviously the people had not actually died but been alive to tell their stories. Although I could see why this had been argued, I didn't completely agree, as I knew from clinical experience that death was a continuum and certainly in the early phases was potentially reversible. That was why we tried to resuscitate patients after their heart had stopped. When somebody died, or in effect had a cardiac arrest, there was a period in which the vital organs, particularly the heart and lungs, could be restarted. If a significant period of time passed, however, then the vital organs would develop permanent damage due to a lack of nutrients, particularly oxygen and glucose, and this would be irreversible and would lead to 'death'. This is the death we usually describe when talking in lay terms.

---

1. The response of pupils to light is mediated by a reflex that is situated in the brain stem, a structure situated at the base of the brain that is involved with vital life processes such as regulating breathing and heartbeat. When the brain stem stops working, this reflex is lost. In cardiac arrest, it is lost but drugs may be administered, such as epinephrine and atropine, that can also make the pupils look large and fixed and hence confuse the issue. We know, however, from the loss of other reflexes, such as the gag reflex (the reflex in the throat that stops food or other materials from going down the windpipe), when this vital part of the brain isn't working.

During the next few months we began to develop Dr Fenwick's original idea into a more global study of NDE in cardiac arrest. Throughout this time Dr Fenwick and I kept in close touch and discussed all the various aspects of the study together.

The first aim of the study was to determine what experiences, if any, people had during a period of clinical death using cardiac arrest as a model. Obviously NDEs had been described for many years but we could not be sure that what people experienced during a cardiac arrest would actually correspond to that description. People might have no experiences or even completely different experiences. This needed to be investigated. Nobody had yet done a prospective study (that is, when the patients are followed forward in time), so we didn't know.

The second aim of the study was to determine the frequency of NDEs (should they have occurred) during cardiac arrest, as this had not been investigated before either.

Finally, we wanted to investigate the significance of any NDEs and why they occurred. For this we planned to investigate the three broad theories – brain-based, psychological and transcendental – put forward in the scientific literature.

In February 1997 I started my job at Southampton General, a large hospital with around 1,000 beds and many specialist units, including various intensive care units, such as cardiology and neurology. I was due to rotate through many of the different specialities.

Working as one of the frontline medical staff was very useful, as it meant that I had to deal with critically ill patients on a regular basis. I was the first person to attend the hospital cardiac arrests when I was on call and so I gained experience of managing and resuscitating these patients. I also managed many other medical emergencies on a regular basis, such as heart attacks and respiratory, heart, kidney and liver failure.

In my first post I worked for Professor Cyrus Cooper, a brilliant academic with an incredible memory and all-round knowledge of medicine. He was also a very kind and supportive doctor to work for. One day as we were walking down the corridor, having finished our rounds, I nervously told him of my interest in NDEs and my desire to set up a study in Southampton. To my surprise he showed a lot of interest and became very keen to help. At the end of our conversation he suggested that I speak to the head of the coronary care unit, Dr Derek Waller, and also the head of the emergency services, Dr John Heyworth.

'You won't be able to do this study without Dr Waller and Dr Heyworth's help. Why don't you go and speak to Derek Waller and tell him that I sent you?'

I did, but Dr Waller's first reaction was bewilderment. He just looked at me and said, 'Have you done your MRCP exams yet?'

'No, not yet. I have only just started the medical rotation.'

He looked back at me as if to say, 'Well, don't you think you should do your exams first?'

I thought, *Well, that's that then. He definitely won't support me. He obviously isn't very interested.*

Dr Heyworth was more supportive, however, and agreed to let me use the emergency areas if the study went ahead.

A few weeks later, while working on the ward, I bumped into Dr Waller again. He came up to me and said, 'I was thinking about that idea of yours the other night. Have you thought about it any further?'

I was taken aback, but also very happy that he had raised the subject with me again.

'Well, yes ... I would like to do the study if possible and I wanted to ask if you would mind helping me with it.'

The whole thing obviously sounded a little strange to him, but after I had explained it in more detail, he agreed to help. As time went on, he also took more of an interest and started telling me of discussions that he had had with other medical colleagues and their views.

With his support, we submitted an application to the local ethics committee and to my delight got a letter back saying 'Approved'! We had taken a huge step forward, as we now had formal permission to start the study.

As the summer approached I wrote to all the other senior doctors in the medical unit of the hospital and informed them of our intention to start the study and possibly recruit some of their patients. I had replies back from all of them and thankfully no one objected. Some found the whole proposal quite interesting, even entertaining. One wrote back saying, 'No, I have no objection ... This proposal really brightened up a dull Friday afternoon!'

One day while I was talking to Dr Waller about the project, he said, 'I was thinking you should also write to Professor Douglas Chamberlain for some advice regarding the aspects of the study related to the heart. He may be able to help you with that. Also send my regards.'

Douglas Chamberlain was very famous in the world of cardiac arrest and resuscitation. He was a professor of cardiology and for many years had played a leading role in research. His guidelines on cardiac arrest resuscitation management were now standard practice worldwide. To my mind he was something of a medical celebrity. I agreed to write to him, but didn't really expect a reply. I thought at best I would get a standard response saying, 'Thank you for your letter, but no, thank you.' However, a week later I had a very interesting letter back from Professor Chamberlain in which he related the case of a man he had resuscitated many years earlier while working as an army doctor. It had happened in 1960, just around the time when modern resuscitation techniques were being developed, and Professor Chamberlain had of course played a leading role in this. One day, after prescribing a drip to a patient on the ward, he had gone to clinic when the head nurse called him back to the ward in a rush:

'On my arrival the patient did not have a pulse, so I started resuscitation. Techniques were more primitive then, but I persevered and then continued until eventually the patient's heart restarted. The man eventually made a full recovery and then started to tell me that during the resuscitation process he had been at the ceiling watching me working on him. He also went on to tell me that without wanting to sound ungrateful, he really didn't want to come back! ... We later discovered that the manufacturer of the drips had supplied contaminated products and this had caused his cardiac arrest.'

I hadn't expected this! I guess it wasn't really surprising, though. Professor Chamberlain had dealt with many cardiac arrest patients, so it was understandable that he had encountered a patient with an NDE. But his perspective gave me a new insight. This was the first time that I had come across an NDE case recounted by a doctor looking after a patient. (In the following years other cases followed from specialist doctors looking after critically ill patients.)

We were almost there now. We had all the permission we needed to start. As this was a very new type of study and had not been performed before, we decided to conduct it on a small scale, essentially as a pilot to start with, and then, depending on the results, perhaps take it further. We actually had no choice about this – Dr Fenwick had around £3,000–5,000 in his research budget that wasn't being used and that was all we had for the whole study!

The plan was to identify all the people who had suffered a cardiac arrest on the emergency, coronary care and medical units of the hospital and had survived. They would be interviewed as soon as possible afterwards, typically within two to five days, and would be asked if they had any memories from the period of cardiac arrest. The interviews had to be done within a few days as there was evidence from psychological studies that people could start to falsely construct events in their minds as time went on. During the interviews, we would in no way mention anything related to death or dying or NDEs, or anything that might suggest those issues to them. The question would be very simple: 'Do you remember anything from the period in which you were unconscious?' If a patient replied, 'Yes,' we would then allow them to describe the experience in more detail and would give the experience a score based upon the Greyson scale. This would allow us to define the experience either as an NDE or not. It would also provide us with a measure of the depth of the experience.

Those patients with an NDE would be placed in one study group and those without in another group. The two groups would thus be the same, particularly from a biological point of view, as they had both had a cardiac arrest and reached the point of clinical death, except that one group had experienced an NDE while the other had not. This way we had a well-matched group which would act as a 'control' for those who had had an NDE.

Data would then be gathered from the medical records regarding each patient's oxygen, carbon dioxide, sodium and potassium levels, and these would be compared to see if there were any differences between those who had had an NDE and those who had not. We would also look at any differences in the drugs administered to the two groups. I was particularly interested in the oxygen levels, both to test the 'dying brain' theory and to examine whether a lack of oxygen played a significant role in causing NDEs.

During the study, we would also ask patients about their religious beliefs to see if there was a relationship between people's religious backgrounds and their near death experiences. For example, would Christians have a different NDE from atheists and non-Christians? This would test some of the psychological theories.

The final aspect of the study would be to test the claims of those who had had out of body experiences. The original idea that Dr

Fenwick had was to place different symbols such as crosses on the top of hospital monitors in each room so that they would only be visible from above. The problem with monitors, though, was that they usually tilted downwards and so it was impossible to place figures or images on them that were truly not visible from below. Therefore an alternative method was needed.

I thought back to the envelope that Dr Fenwick had originally used to show me his idea. *We should simply replicate that,* I thought. I also discussed my ideas with another distinguished doctor. He said, 'You should use different images such as writing, pictures, newspaper articles, etc.' That seemed like a very good idea, as it would obviously be much harder for a patient to have imagined the detail that would be needed to identify a newspaper article or a picture than a simple cross. We therefore decided to prepare special boards and place an image or writing on them.

The head of health and safety at the hospital insisted that our boards were fireproof and the only material that we could find which was definitely going to be acceptable, as it was already hanging all over the hospital, was the material that the ceiling tiles were made of. We therefore purchased some 150 of these tiles and had a local print company attach the pictures, images and newspaper articles onto them. We also had to purchase a special type of hanging material and clips that would allow us to hang the tiles from the ceiling. The whole cost of preparing these items was around £1,500. Before we were due to set the study up I had to collect and store the tiles; the material was very friable, so you can imagine what a mess they made of both my car and the room!

Finally, we were ready to start. The excitement that morning was truly palpable. We had to cover all the images up, so that when we took the boards onto the wards no one would know what was on them. We especially had to ensure that none of the staff or patients could see what was on them, as that would have invalidated the study. I was really very strict about this aspect, because if a member of staff had seen what was on the boards and someone had identified it, then we would never have known whether that staff member had told the patient or whether the patient had really identified it themselves.

I arrived at the hospital with Tony, the freelance science producer. He wasn't producing a programme this time, he was just going to be a cameraman and record how we set the study up. He had kindly agreed to do this free of charge, as he had a professional camera and was interested in the study.

I had lots of other help too. There were three visiting German medical students, two of my friends, George and Dylon, joined us later that day from London, and even my mother came to Southampton too. We had the mammoth task of covering up all 150 boards and then taking them round to each of the eight wards, plus the coronary care unit and the emergency areas, including the resuscitation room. The aim was to place a target between every two beds so that something would be visible from every corner of the room and above every bed. Where would people claim to have looked down from? Would they claim to have gone up just a few inches or right up to the ceiling? We obviously didn't know and so we had to cover all areas of the room.

Setting up the targets took the entire weekend, but by Sunday evening we had installed all 150 on the wards. When it was all finished, we heaved a great sigh of relief and walked down the corridor feeling exhausted but very pleased with what we had done.

As we walked down, I took a last glance back at the wards we had just left. It was a strange feeling. These were the wards that I had worked on every day for the past six months and they were now the first ever wards anywhere in the world to have been fitted with a huge number of boards with an image facing upwards to test NDEs. But as I turned round and carried on walking out of the hospital, I knew that the real work was just beginning.

3

What Is It Like to Die?

Soon afterwards, I quickly learned two very important lessons in life. First, I learned never to give someone a piece of information and then ask them not to tell other people – well, at least not unless I wanted everyone to know! Second, I learned that although research is wonderful, as soon as it starts, it becomes a great test of patience and mental endurance!

Two months had passed by since we had installed the targets on the wards and everything was going well – except for the fact that nobody had had an NDE! Still, we had weathered the initial worries and concerns and I generally felt more comfortable with the study. The first few weeks after we had installed the targets, I had gone through a period of worry. Every day I used to feel really uneasy about what I would find when I walked into work. Although we had tested the strength of the boards and the connections as we had set them up, I still worried about whether one of them would fall down in the night. That was in fact my biggest fear!

The boards really were an eyesore and so it would have been impossible not to draw attention to them. We had told everyone on the wards that they were for a study, but hadn't told them the details.

If anyone asked, I used to say, 'It is to do with dust collection.' The only people who had been informed of the real reason for having the boards were the senior nurses who were in charge of the wards and the senior doctors – in total perhaps around 20 people. I had asked them all to be discreet and not to tell anybody else the reason for having the boards. I had particularly emphasized this to the senior nurses on each ward and had suggested that if anyone asked, they were simply to say they were for a study to do with dust collection.

Unfortunately, one evening one of the nurses who knew about the boards decided to tell another nurse. I later heard about their conversation and it had gone something like this:

'Do you know what these boards are actually for?'

'Yes, I think they are for a study to do with indoor dust.'

'No, they are actually to test people who may have had out of body experiences!'

'What? What do you mean? What are you talking about?'

'Really, they are there in case someone describes being out of body! Trust me … If you don't believe me, then take a look!'

That obviously caused a lot of excitement and broke the monotony of the night shift! The nurses started calling around all the other wards telling others what the boards were really for! I can only imagine the shock on their faces. During the next few weeks some nurses climbed onto chairs, stools and even stepladders to try to see exactly what was on the boards! One day one of them even broke one of the boards as she leaned over to look at it! When I asked her about the shattered board hanging from the ceiling, she initially insisted, 'It just happened spontaneously,' but once I explained that none of the other boards had broken or even come loose, she confessed and apologized. During the setting-up phase we had thought of many possible outcomes with the boards, but not that they would have to take the weight of a person! They really weren't designed for that sort of thing!

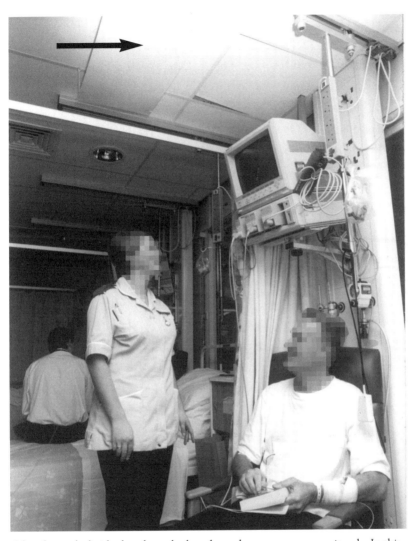

After the study finished we kept the boards on the coronary care unit only. In this picture, in the corner of the coronary care unit, above the bed, you can see a white board hanging from the ceiling (*arrow*). This is an example of the second version of the targets, which actually blended in with the ceiling and so drew far less attention. On the surface facing the ceiling various images were attached. The first version of the boards had been made of inverted ceiling tiles, which were a real 'eyesore'! It was one of these first ones that was broken by an over-curious nurse one night! The second version was made of plastic and so was a lot easier to manage. I used to clean these boards and change the images regularly, even though I have never been really keen on heights! We kept the boards suspended for over three years waiting to set up a larger study, but in the end we had them removed until a newer study could be set up.

News of the study soon trickled down from the ward nurses to the student nurses, medical students and even to the hospital volunteers who served tea and coffee. Before long everyone knew about the study. One day, when a student nurse was asked by a patient what the board hanging over his head was for, she replied, 'Oh, that's in case you have an out of body experience, sir!' It really wasn't very good at all! I had been extremely naïve and now I was paying the price for it.

Though I really wasn't very happy about all the interest, there was very little I could do at that point. I just had to wait and let the excitement settle. I also had to assume that all our writing and pictures had been seen and hence invalidated. So we had a big problem! The only way around it would be to install new images once all the interest had died down. In the meantime I just carried on with the study. We could still collect data about NDEs, as the only area that had been compromised had been any potential out of body claims. Eventually, in the months that followed, I replaced all the pictures very discreetly while 'cleaning' the boards during my weekends off. This was something I had to do on a number of occasions. I also made sure that no two boards had similar images.

By this time things had all begun to fit into a simple routine. We had employed a very bright nurse to help us with the study. Her name was Becky and she had worked as a nurse at the hospital before and had now gone to university to study for a Master's degree. This was ideal for her as it meant she could work part time. She was extremely keen and enthusiastic, conducted most of the interviews and helped us enormously throughout the study.

Every day we used to check whether there had been a cardiac arrest in the hospital and if so, where. This was done through the hospital switchboard, as they had an accurate record of every cardiac arrest call that was put out. Some days there had been no cardiac arrests and some days there had been many. After identifying a specific ward, we would then go there and find out who had had the cardiac arrest and whether or not they had survived. Since only 20 per cent of cardiac arrest patients would have been expected to survive, the vast majority had not survived, but if they had we would check to see whether they were medically fit enough to be approached. Usually they would not be well enough for at least a few days, although if the cardiac arrest had been short-lived, they could speak sooner.

When they were well enough to speak, we would say to them: 'We are trying to understand more about what people experience when they are in a deep coma. I understand you were in a severe coma a few days ago. Do you remember anything from the time in which you were in a coma? Do you have any specific memories?'

Most people would at this point look at me in a strange way as if to say, 'Well, what kind of doctor are you? Of course not – I was in a coma!' After that they would just say, 'No.'

We would then look at their medical records and take down the relevant information regarding their oxygen levels, carbon dioxide levels and sodium and potassium levels in the blood from the time of the cardiac arrest. These were our control group of subjects.

Things were progressing nicely until one day I had a call out of the blue.

'Is that Dr Parnia?'

'Yes.'

'Are you the doctor who is doing a study into dying and out of body experiences?'

'Yes.'

'Oh, I've been looking all over for you – I am glad that I've found you! I am Marilyn from the hospital public relations office. I have had a number of enquiries from the local press about your study. They are very interested in your work and have been calling me up, desperately looking to interview you.'

Oh no! I thought. That was all I needed! In hindsight of course I shouldn't have been too surprised by the call. There had been so much talk inside the hospital that it was only a matter of time before the news spread out into the community. But I really didn't want any further publicity.

'I am not at all keen to speak to them. I don't want to speak about the study until it has been completed.'

'Well, that's up to you. I can tell them that if you want, but the problem is that they already know there is something going on in the hospital, so if you don't speak to them then they will write something anyway and it may be very inaccurate. This way at least you have a chance to tell them what you want them to know.'

I could see that Marilyn had a good point. It would be in our best interest to give the correct information. So I agreed to hold a press conference at the hospital. I was really afraid of getting all the wrong headlines anyway, but I really didn't have a lot of choice in the matter.

That day I was interviewed by two reporters from the local newspapers and a local BBC radio reporter. Thankfully it went very well. In fact the press were very good and respected my concerns regarding the need to keep certain aspects of the work – particularly the boards – vague.

As time went on I felt much more comfortable talking to the press and took part in a number of other interviews. At the end of one of the interviews on national TV, it was announced that those who had had an NDE could write to me at the hospital. I didn't know what to expect, but I waited in anticipation.

The following day I received 40–50 letters and I continued to receive letters regularly for almost two weeks afterwards. At the end of this time I had received reports of almost 250 NDEs and out of body experiences from the community. After other press interviews, other people also wrote to me. In total I collected in excess of 500 cases that year.

These letters were truly enlightening. While the cardiac arrest study went on, I concentrated on reading them. Up until then my knowledge of NDEs had been based on what I had read in books or scientific publications. These first-hand accounts provided a real eye-opener and took my understanding of the subject much further.

Many of the people who wrote to me also accepted my request to attend for an interview at the hospital and so I was able to study their accounts in detail. During this time I became even more astonished and touched by the mystery of near death experiences and the profound effect they had on those who experienced them. Many of the people I met, or who sent their accounts to me, had been positively transformed by their experiences and had done astonishingly humane things afterwards.

It became quite clear that there was a common thread to the experience. These accounts seemed to confirm Moody's original description that coming close to death was a largely pleasant experience for the majority. Certainly the people who had written to me commonly described feeling peaceful and joyous, seeing a bright light, seeing a tunnel, seeing deceased relatives, entering a heavenly domain, reaching a point of no return and having a life review, as well as separating from the body and watching events from above. Importantly for many, they had now lost their fear of death and had been positively transformed, drawing inspiration from their experience to go on and perform altruistic work with a sense of humility. I learned so much from all the people who shared their experiences with me.

One of the most consistent features that I came across was a great sense of calm and peace, which for the majority of people occurred in the early stages of the experience and then lasted throughout the NDE. In many cases people described becoming pain-free, calm and peaceful before going on to have the near death experience. One woman wrote:

'I suffered a gynaecological haemorrhage and was admitted as
an emergency to hospital … It happened again … this time it
was worse, and I was lying in a pool of blood. The doctor was
called and there was a lot of urgent activity around my bed …
That was the last thing I remembered. Then I was high on
the ceiling of the ward looking down upon the bed (which
seemed to be a long way down) and saw the doctors and
nurses around the bed working on the person lying there.
I was surrounded by a strong light. I did not go through any
tunnels. I was not frightened – in fact I was very happy, very
peaceful and in awe of the wonderful light all around me.
The light was so beautiful – brighter than the clearest
sunshine and yet not dazzling. I had never seen such light
before and never felt such peace.'

Many other people also described an out of body experience as
well as the sensation of seeing a bright warm welcoming light.
The out of body experience was described as a sensation of separating
from the body and being able to watch themselves and events that
were taking place from a point above. Once in an out of body state,
people typically described feeling very 'light' and 'peaceful'. I noticed
that they often inadvertently described themselves as the part that
had separated from the body. For example, they would say, '*I* was at
the corner of the ceiling, looking down at *my* body. While at the
ceiling *I* thought to myself, *What is my body doing down there?*' The 'I'
part was always the part at the ceiling and not the other way round.

Many recalled very specific details about events that had actually
taken place during their experience. One woman explained:

'… during my operation I was floating around the operating
theatre. I could see the surgeon and nurses working on my
body, although I cannot now remember how many people

there were. I could also hear their conversation ... the
surgeon said he would leave the wound open to let it drain
as the appendix had burst. He then visited me on the ward
afterwards to explain what he had done and I already knew as
I had heard him. He said I couldn't possibly have heard him
and suggested that a nurse had been to my bedside and told
me ... I did not tell him I had seen the operation being
performed ...'

As well as highlighting the ability to recall 'seeing' specific details
and describing the self as the part that had detached from the body,
this woman's case also illustrated the common reaction of disbelief
from the medical and nursing staff when told about specific things
that they had said or done. Another woman wrote:

'I was pregnant ... in and out of hospital because I had a
blood disorder ... The blood was pouring out of me during the
delivery and I had to have 24 stitches ... I can remember so
vividly being above and to the right of the bed in the delivery
room at the head end in a white-like tunnel, but it was white,
absolutely brilliant white ... I looked down and I could see Dr
Gallagher, I could see what he was doing and I saw him run
round the bottom end of the delivery bed ... he must have
forgotten [a bucket] was there because I saw him kick it in his
haste to get round the other side and he kicked this bucket
and it knocked into a trolley with all the instruments on,
things like bowls, etc., and that trolley whizzed across the
room and hit the wall. It didn't tip right up but you could see
things falling off it and he then came round to me on my left-
hand side and I saw him thumping on my chest, thumping
and thumping. I heard nothing, I could see nothing, no sound
whatsoever, I just saw what he was doing ... It was peace, it

was peace, it was absolute peace … I just looked down at myself … I could possibly say it was a tunnel where you were looking down [from], but all this light was around you, it was a brilliant light … and then there was a noise, a terrible noise … I just said, "Let me go back, it was beautiful …" The next day I spoke to the doctor and I was telling him what he had done and he was furious and wanted to know which nurse had told me!'

There were many similar cases in which the individual described an interest in the events that had been going on around them. Another woman wrote:

'This experience occurred following a complication of the delivery of a child … I saw myself lying flat in the bed, surrounded by different monitors and drips. I felt myself "float" over to the monitors on the other side of the room, looking at the data on screen. At the time I could not take in what the monitors were showing, despite my medical background. I then "floated" over to where the nurse was standing near a board. She was writing at the time, and I looked over her shoulder. Again I had difficulty in understanding what exactly was the problem with me. But during this time I did not feel frightened or threatened, but I knew who I was …'

The people who wrote to me were not necessarily religious. Here is the account of someone who described herself as a 'practical, non-religious' nurse. She had been admitted to hospital for an operation to remove her womb and had had an internal haemorrhage afterwards:

'I was awake and aware of my surroundings. A nurse came in to take my blood pressure every half-hour. On one occasion I remember her taking my blood pressure and then running out of the room, which I thought was unusual. I don't remember anything more after that consciously, but I was then aware of being above my body as if I was floating on the ceiling and looking down at myself in the hospital bed with a crowd of doctors and nurses around me. It seemed clear that there was something wrong, but I don't think I had had a cardiac arrest because I was not aware of anybody jumping up and down on my chest or doing any resuscitation. I could hear people talking about me and there was some concern. This seemed to go on for probably about 5–10 minutes, I would think, then I think there was a blank period again because the next thing I remember was actually … waking up still in the same bed and seeing people in hospital theatre gowns standing around me. I asked them what they were doing and they explained that I had some bleeding and that they were looking for the signs of the bleeding ... it took me by surprise, as I don't have any religious beliefs or position on the afterlife. At that stage I had never heard of that sort of experience … I was quite surprised to have what appeared to be a sort of mystical experience, because I don't believe in ghosts or spiritual experiences at all. I subsequently discovered by looking at my own chart that my blood pressure had been recorded at 50/0, so obviously I'd had a fairly massive internal bleed!'

Some people described leaving the body as being like taking off an item of clothing or shedding a layer of skin. A man from New Zealand who had been involved in a road traffic accident wrote:

'When I came to, someone was holding me down on the road and I was having a lot of difficulty breathing ... I lapsed into unconsciousness again and revived partially once more in the Intensive Care Unit ... I realise now that this must have been very soon after the accident. I knew I was in a different existence and in my unconscious state I remember thinking, "So this is dying." I never thought it was so easy. It was like taking off your coat ... The one thing that stood out was that my spirit moved separately from my body ... In some strange way, however, it was still part of me.'

Although the majority of people described being able to observe events in the vicinity of their body, some described viewing events beyond their own environment. A man with a heart attack recalled:

'I was rushed into hospital with severe pain in my left arm and jaws ... I had a heart attack. The next thing I remember I was flying outside the hospital grounds over people and cars. I was lifted up over two rows of trees into the sky, between two beams of light. I was aware that I was on my journey up. It was not until I came to a sudden halt that I was gripped by fear. I called out loud, "Oh well, there is nothing I can do now, I can't get back." I remember being afraid to look back. Then I was taken further up. I came to a halt. I saw ... there were billions of stars ... Then I found myself awake in my hospital bed ... The doctor said, "I am afraid we lost you and had to pump electricity through you."'

Others described being attached to the body by a line or a cord:

'I remember the out of body experience I had as a child of eleven ... I was not at all frightened. In fact I felt at home, but also aware I couldn't stay out of the body too long. I could see I was attached to a thin line, a sort of lifeline, but I also saw the doctor who was dressed in the white coat busy at some machine …'

Many people described seeing a tunnel during their NDE. This was depicted in different ways. The majority described it as a long dark tunnel, but others described it in other ways, such as a kaleidoscope or a tunnel with coloured tiles on the sides. After actually talking to the people it became clear that although in some cases their descriptions seemed different, they all seemed to be referring to the same concept. Often people also described seeing a bright light at the end of the tunnel, which was usually portrayed as being bright, warm and welcoming.

Some people simply saw a tunnel, while others described actually going through it. The sensation of travelling through the tunnel was at times described as simple movement and at other times as being pulled through. Those who described going through the tunnel sometimes recalled arriving in a beautiful garden-like place. In many cases the sensation of going through the tunnel was associated with other NDE features, such as encountering a being of light or seeing deceased relatives at the end of the tunnel. One person wrote:

'I … went into anaphylactic shock. I "died" and saw all the old relatives who have passed on. There was a large tunnel and all these people were calling me to join them. I started to go towards them and then my husband came and found me and revived me …'

Another wrote:

'I was floating or flying down a tunnel. People were beckoning me to keep going … when suddenly I came out of the tunnel into a beautiful light, a garden of lovely bright colours which disappeared very quickly and I was back in the hospital bed …'

Another person described the tunnel walls:

'I remember going down a tunnel. It was dark on the top and bottom, but not solid. The sides were like tiles – some were red, yellow and green, the others were black. All had a shine to them … The feeling of the experience was very calming, relaxing and tranquil.'

Some described hearing a voice during the NDE or seeing a person who told them they could not go further and should go back. Others described a voluntary decision not to go through the tunnel. For many the driving force that made them return was that they had to care for people who were dependent on them. This was a very beautiful and poignant feature that is illustrated in the following case:

'… in my forties I had a serious car accident … I regained consciousness as I was being put in the ambulance … I then had a three-hour operation with three surgeons … I appeared to be looking down on my body lying on the bed with doctors and nurses on both sides of the bed attending to me. I was floating on clouds, pink tinged, like looking out of an aircraft, with a tunnel of bright light, but although it was peaceful and pleasant I remembered my children and panicked to get to them … I then returned to my body and heard one of the nurses say, "That was a near thing."'

Another person wrote:

'I felt myself [rise] above, hovering over the bed, up to the
ceiling, looking down on myself in a blue light. I saw the
doctors and nurses all around my bed and there were quite a
few of them … I had no pain at all. To the right of the room
up high I sensed a tunnel of light, but I didn't want to go
through it, as I had just had my little girl and wanted to
go back and look after her, and my husband and parents.
I remember drift-ing back down into my body and back, oh,
painfully back …'

Some had felt themselves being pulled into the tunnel but resisted
it, as they felt it wasn't their turn yet. A road traffic accident victim
wrote:

'I was given excellent treatment in the trauma unit … In the
early hours of the first or second morning they could not
stabilise me … I do not have any recollection of my condition
or the events that happened in hospital … but I do recall
quite clearly an experience that is very hard to put into
words … I felt a gravity, a force pulling me into a blackness.
I could not move and was totally fixed on the blackness that
was pulling me in. It had a presence unlike anything else you
can imagine and I didn't want to go! With all my strength
and will I tried to turn away. I was shouting in my head over
and over, "No, no, it's not my time!" It seemed to take
forever, but eventually my head started to move away. The
force was strong and it took more effort than I can describe,
but I did it and the more I turned away, the easier it became,
until I felt a release from the pull. I then felt myself floating
and as I span completely away from the force I saw the most

gorgeous light I have ever seen. It was a huge orb of light and colour and it was the planet Earth. I was in space miles above gazing down in amazement at the wisps of cloud and blue oceans ...'

As well as the features of an NDE, this case also illustrates a very important point. After a significant insult to the brain, such as occurs with a head injury, a seizure or a change in blood oxygen, carbon dioxide or glucose levels, there is normally a period of memory loss before and after the insult. This lasts for a variable length of time, ranging from a few minutes to many days or weeks, and is due to an imbalance in the normal biology required for the brain to function. The extent of memory loss depends on the severity of the insult. In this case, as in many others, there was memory loss for the events that had occurred before and after the insult (a head injury), as well as for the events that had taken place during the illness. However, despite this there was 'complete' recall of the NDE.

For many people the light at the end of the tunnel started out dim and then gradually increased in intensity. It was typically bright, but did not hurt the eye. It was described as 'warm' and 'welcoming' and it drew the individual to it. It often left them with a real sense of warmth and a feeling of being loved.

Those who encountered this light often described undergoing a powerful transformation and experiencing a dramatic change in their mindset. Typically, people felt that they had become less material-istic, kinder to others, more of service, less afraid of death and generally more pious and religious. In some cases their family mem-bers had also noticed a change. Some people who had been atheists developed a very strong faith in God. The effect typically lasted for decades.

Some also encountered a 'being of light', either at the end of the tunnel or as they travelled through it. The being emanated love, compassion and warmth and made the person feel very welcome and loved. It often played the role of an educator gently taking the person through a review of their life in which they could both see what they had done and understand what mistakes they had made. The aim seemed to be to educate and guide them, though they may have felt the pain and discomfort that they had caused others as a way of understanding why their actions had been wrong. The majority of those who had had an NDE had no doubt that it was a vision of death and beyond.

Many also described how communication took place in a non-verbal manner, almost as if by telepathy.

As well as seeing a being of light, people described seeing deceased relatives during their NDE, usually parents, although in some cases it was another member of the family. Some people described seeing friends instead or even people they did not know. Sometimes the relative or other person welcomed them, and in many cases appeared to be expecting them, and at other times they told them to go back, as it was not their time to die yet. A man wrote:

> 'In June 1996 my wife and I had been out for the day and got home about 5 p.m. I went upstairs to the toilet and coming out of the toilet, as I opened the door, I had a tremendous pain in my chest ... All I can recall now is the terrible pain I was in and a banging on my chest. This suddenly stopped – no more chest pain, no banging on my chest. I was floating on a big ball of white clouds surrounded by beautiful golden scenery. The whole scene was extremely bright and clear and suddenly my brother appeared with his usual smile and I called to him, "Hi, Monty." He had died six months earlier of a heart attack.'

The following case is of a woman who described seeing a being of light and some of the deceased members of her family as well:

'My own experience began after coming around from the operation, with tubes attached to me … I became aware of the surgeon and anaesthetist standing at the foot of my bed. The conversation went like this: Surgeon: "Well, we have done all we can. This little lady doesn't know which way to go, so we will leave her alone and let her decide which way she's going." In the quiet and peace that followed, my spirit left my body and I travelled down this tunnel leading towards a bright light at the end. It seemed to be a long way away. I couldn't wait to get there. When I reached the end Jesus stood there with his arms open wide and stopped me, then said, "Not this time, I have more work for you to do, you must go back." At this point my husband and father (both had previously died) came towards me in the spirit and guided me back.'

In the following case a woman gave a detailed account of meeting a 'perfect being', who then guided her through her experience. When I interviewed her she said that she found it difficult to convey the feelings of deep compassion, love and kindness that had emanated from the being:

'It all came to a head when I collapsed at home and crawled to a telephone. I had a friend who came to my aid and I was eventually admitted to hospital … I had not had anything to drink for 48 hours as any food increased the pain, so my medical condition was not very good … My problem was that I was suffering with an ectopic pregnancy, the tube [fallopian] was rupturing, causing bleeding … I suddenly found myself standing beside myself looking at a cord which connected me to my body and thinking how thin and wispy it was. Someone was beside me. I was made to feel secure and encouraged to trust my companion, who suggested that the cord was insignificant and that I should not concern myself with its fragility. I was guided towards the light. This was a sort of void, in which I found myself with the ability to fly, or should I say I had no weight – a very strange experience. Throughout the journey I kept looking back to ensure my companion was with me but somehow towards the end of the journey I found myself just content to move on and reach the end.

'Reaching the light, I was met by other beings of light and very gently encouraged to move on towards a life review. In this experience my actions were not judged by others, I judged myself. My presence could see into my mind and there was no way I could hide any thoughts. Gently I was encouraged to understand how my mistakes hurt others by experiencing what others had felt as a result of my actions. I was confused, as it all seemed so strange. The word "death" was never mentioned yet somehow I came to understand that I was in that place of spirit where the newly dead move on to. Many questions sprang to mind like how, why? I just had abdominal pain, nothing considered life-threatening. I was told by those in spirit that I had been pregnant. I did not know that I had been pregnant before this; I had just thought that I had abdominal pain. I was also told that the spirit of the child had initially consented to be born and then changed its mind … that it had experienced a very traumatic life before and just could not face life again just yet. Perhaps with love and encouragement it would in the future. I asked to see this spirit and explain that with me and my husband it would have known love. We had been hoping for another baby for some time. There was hesitancy and after a delay one can only assume the spirit concerned was consulted. We spoke together. Poor soul, I really sensed the fear. It felt secure with the brothers around it, who supported it with love ... "One day" was the message from the brothers of light. "Be patient with him."

'I was moved forward and eventually met the great God in many religions, a beautiful experience and I can only say that I fully understand why St Paul so wished to be with him, to be in the presence of such unconditional love, humour ... understanding ... I did not need to speak – thoughts were sufficient. It was as if all were one and shared in his being; his radiance was everywhere. To this day I still look back with elation at this experience.

'I became very distressed and became very concerned at leaving a young 18-month-old baby behind. Who would care for her? My husband was away, no family close by. [God's] compassion was so strong, his love and caring so abundant that by his grace I was allowed to return. I was told that I would have a very special mission to do later in life, when my children grew up. He already knew there would be another.

'I cannot remember much about the return. I recall being at the ceiling of the room and watching two nurses either side of me, working on drips and drains. There was a jolt and in no time I had drifted into what can only be described as sleep.

'I had never read of near death or out of body experiences, terms used today ... Two years later my son was born, very sickly, but to this day I have kept my promise given to him in that world of spirit – that I would love him unconditionally as long as he needed me. I created a home of love and as a family we work together to love each other and the world –

a small mirror of what I experienced in that land of light.
After this experience I have no fear of death and believe with
certainty in the afterlife.'

This was the most complete NDE that I had come across.
The most outstanding feature of this case was probably the woman's
interaction with the being of light. When I met her she told me that
during the process of judgement she felt uncomfortable and
remorseful about the opportunities she had failed to make use of in
her life. She described these opportunities as the situations in which
she could have been a source of goodness for others, but had
neglected to be. She felt that her life had been an opportunity to
develop further. The worst feeling was of having been given a
wonderful opportunity and not using it. She told me that she now
hated to do any harm to others, as she had felt the pain that she had
caused others. She had felt the effects of all her actions on others.

Although when I met her many years had passed since her
experience, it was still fresh in her memory and had had a very
positive effect. She now felt that the most important thing in life was
to take the opportunities to be of assistance to others, even if these
were sometimes the more difficult options. This response also highlights the positive transformation that many people undergo
following an NDE, particularly those who have encountered a being
of light.

A man wrote:

'It happened 17 years ago. I was knocked from my bicycle and
shattered my skull into nine separate fragments and broke my
right arm and my shoulder. I was not expected to live …
I knew there was going to be a tremendous impact a split-
second before the collision that threw me from my bicycle
onto my head in the road. Then I remember nothing until, in

the coma, I went where dead people go. I was standing next to a figure the same height as me. I was standing on his right and he had his right arm across my shoulders. We were looking straight ahead of us into the near distance.

'I have since described this figure as a guide because I found it so hard to say I met God. But it was God – "my" God. As I looked at him he impressed on me that I was seeing the God I was brought up to envisage – he was manifesting in the way most comfortable and acceptable to me. I knew that the grey-haired white-robed, non-sexual (by that I mean he was man and woman or neither) being beside me would be everything to all "dead people". We were standing on what looked like sun-kissed clouds or snow which formed a vast circle … "This is the love held for you by souls already," [he said] … and there appeared a cluster of spheres of light opposite. Human-sized, oval-shaped and the most beautiful pink golden hue that I can only describe as the colour of beams of evening sun … All dead loved ones were there, and the sphere at the forefront was bigger, as it was my grandparents, who were one … The spheres were unrecognizable, as they were all the same, but I knew who was who. "God" told me to look down below … and way below us was Earth. "This is the love held for you by those on Earth," I was told … Throughout my experience I was told I wasn't to stay and that I was being shown this to sustain me through my life, which has been very hard. I came back into my body through a tunnel …'

In their letters many people described entering a very beautiful place in which they felt very happy, content and peaceful, and which they often did not want to leave. The descriptions of the place ranged from misty surroundings to a beautiful meadow, a garden or grassland.

One woman wrote:

'I've suffered with asthma for many years and have been hospitalised and had close calls several times, but this time was different … I went through a tunnel … When I came out of the tunnel I was in a pearly, misty place … It was then that I thought, "I've died." But to make sure, I went back to my body. There was no heartbeat, no breath, I couldn't make it move or speak, so I concluded, "Yeah, definitely dead," and went back into the pearly place where I reminded myself there was nothing to fear. At that instant I was in a different level. Here all was soft gold, including me … all of life's fears and worries seemed so unimportant, so absolutely nothing to worry about, and all our fearful fretting seemed so unnecessary … I was aware that behind me stretched infinity, that all the people I'd ever known, knew now and even would know were there, all made out of this golden "light", all made of the same stuff, and so truly we are all one. I saw this like a liquid golden ocean out of which each person rose, made of the ocean, in their own individual shape, but all one originally, basically. Many loved ones were there and endless joy.'

Another woman who found herself in a beautiful place wrote:

'Early in August 1976, after having a hysterectomy … I started to haemorrhage badly. I was still unconscious at this point from the effects of the anaesthetic, so I knew nothing of what happened until the next day … I was told later that my heart had stopped before they could get me back down to the theatre and they had tried to resuscitate me. They had finally got me back into theatre and had to cut into my abdomen to see what had gone wrong – it was a vein that had been punctured during the first operation.

'After becoming fully conscious I started to remember what I first thought was a dream where I found myself whizzing through a dark tunnel at great speed and I could see a blinding bright light at the end of it. When finally I came out of it, I found myself looking at a beautiful meadow. There was a young woman standing behind a traditional wooden five-barred gate. She was wearing a white dress and a circlet of fresh flowers on her head. She kept telling me that I had to go back, that it was too soon for me to be there and that there were things I had to do still in my life. I felt quite bereft at this, but at the back of my mind I remembered that I had three children, the youngest of whom was two years old, and a wonderful husband, and I knew I couldn't leave them at that point. Then it was all over and I don't remember how I got back into my body. The next thing I recalled was waking up, looking at the clock, which read five o'clock, and thinking, "Oh no, I haven't been to theatre yet, after having waited all afternoon …" It was of course the following morning, which took a few minutes to register!

'The lady that I remembered seeing was someone I knew as a young girl. She was a couple of years older than me and went to the same school, and we also went to the same riding stables. Maureen was always messing about with electrical things and was told many times by different people at the stables in my hearing that she would kill herself one day. Sadly it happened two years after she had her first child, a lovely little girl. I was on my way home one Saturday night and stopped to buy something from a local shop. Maureen was there with her daughter and we chatted for a few minutes. I hadn't seen her for a few years then. Two weeks

later, again a Saturday evening, I bought a local paper and on
the front page was a picture of Maureen and the headlines
that she had died trying to change a plug on a kettle.'

This case also demonstrates that those who make a conscious
decision to return often do so because of the need to care for others,
particularly small children. Another interesting feature was that
many people recalled reaching a symbolic point of no return, which
they knew they should not go beyond. In this case, it was a wooden
gate. Others recalled a stream, a river or a doorway. A person who had
suffered severe anaphylactic shock after an abdominal operation
wrote:

'I knew no more of the outside world until I came to – soaked
in perspiration – to see the surgeon and his registrar sitting at
the foot of the bed doing something to my right ankle – a
"cut down" to get fluid into my collapsed system. The surgeon
was suturing the tube into place. He subsequently told me
that he thought he had lost me, it was such a near death
situation.
　'The strange thing was that "inside myself" at the time …
I was busy with my own experience, which was strange.
I became very aware of my own existence … I was then aware
that I was very peaceful and calm and felt that I was "held"
by a Loving Presence at a point in time which was critical.
It can only be described as the "point of no return". I felt very
happy and knew that if I went beyond this point there was
something vital, ongoing, full of life beyond. It was like
waiting for a door to open … I felt entirely alive, alert, myself
and happy – a deep all-pervading sense of content – and
"knew" that beyond that point was something wonderful.
And that is all I remember because I came to in my hospital

bed wondering why the surgeon was playing with my right
foot when he had operated on my abdomen!'

All the accounts that people sent to me were truly enlightening.
Here I have only been able to convey a fraction of them. They were
really moving and I felt very privileged to have had the opportunity
to study them. I was also extremely touched by the wonderful
generosity of all the people who so kindly shared their intimate
secrets with me. It was astonishing to think these accounts represented just a small selection of NDEs from people in the wider
community.

Although I couldn't comment on the validity of people's claims,
obviously the NDEs were very real to those who had experienced
them. No two experiences were exactly the same, but at the very least
the dying process really seemed to be a pleasant experience for the
vast majority of people and seemed to unfold in a particular pattern.

Even though in many cases the critical event or illness that had
led to the NDE had been unpleasant and painful, there appeared to
be a point at which any pain or distress was replaced by peaceful,
pleasant feelings. For many, this then led on to the experience of
seeing and going though a tunnel, typically very fast, towards a bright
light at the end. Some people experienced seeing the light at the
beginning of the experience, while others did not see the tunnel at
all. In many cases people found it difficult to find words to adequately
describe the beauty of the light and the sensations they felt on seeing
it. Those who did describe it typically called it a very 'warm',
'welcoming' and 'glorious' light that did not hurt their eyes but
instead drew them towards it.

Many also described the sensation of separating from their bodies
and being able to 'see' events from below while 'floating' in an 'out of
body' state. This was described as being like removing a heavy
garment of clothing or shedding a skin and moving away freely,

leaving the old skin behind. Interestingly, people consistently described the 'self' as the part that was above, rather than the body that was lying below.

Throughout the experiences people consistently described being able to think clearly and lucidly, with well-structured thought processes together with clear reasoning and memory formation. Essentially, during the NDE people retained largely the same consciousness and personality as they had before the experience, although the experience did change them afterwards.

Some experienced seeing other people, most commonly deceased relatives, friends or even complete strangers. It was almost as if these people had come to greet them and to help them through their experience. Sometimes they saw others as spheres of light, some more glorious than others. Many also felt that all were equal.

Some experienced seeing a 'being of light' who was full of love, mercy and compassion and in their eyes was 'perfect'. This being sometimes played the role of a loving educator, who with kindness and compassion watched over the person and guided them through the experience and in some cases a review of their lives. The prevailing feature during the whole experience was a deep sense of all-pervading love and benevolence. The love that emanated from the being of light had a far deeper intensity than that which emanated from other people who were encountered during the experience. Some identified the being of light as 'God', while others described it as a religious figure such as Jesus, and others still simply thought of it as an unnamed 'being of light'.

During the experience communication took place through 'minds' rather than verbal speech. During their interactions with the being of light some described undergoing a 'review' of their lives. They sometimes found themselves seeing and experiencing all that they had done and felt completely 'transparent' as regards their actions, words and intentions. All that they had thought, felt or experienced was completely and clearly visible to them as well as to the being of light. Some also described being able to feel any pain and distress they had caused others during their lifetime. Therefore they had come to a point where they didn't want to harm others, whether by actions or words. They began to view life as an opportunity to be a source of goodness to others. After the NDE, they described a major transformation in their personalities. This was particularly the case for those who had encountered the being of light. They described losing any fear of death and becoming less materialistic and more altruistic. Many had engaged more in activities that would help others.

Finally, although having a religious theme, NDEs did not seem to correlate directly with traditional religious views of the afterlife. A bright warm welcoming light, a tunnel and a being of light are not typical descriptions of the afterlife in most religions. Nevertheless, there seemed to be an interesting point about the role of an individual's background in interpreting the NDE: people often seemed to interpret their NDE based upon their own underlying thought processes. So, for example, a Christian who saw a being of light would identify it as Jesus, while someone of a different faith would describe it as being a religious figure related to their own faith, while others interpreted it as being God himself and others just called it a 'luminous being'. Despite the different terminology, however, they appeared to be describing the same concept.

For a long while, the only people I came across who had had an NDE were those who had sent in their accounts. Now I needed to see what experiences people would have during the cardiac arrest study. This was the really important group that we needed to study. Sadly, though, most of the people who had cardiac arrests were too ill to survive and those who did had no memories from that period. I was beginning to get despondent, but I had no choice other than to be patient and persevere with the study.

4

The Scientific Paradox

Whether I liked it or not, by this point I had become well known as the doctor researching near death experiences and the 'afterlife' at Southampton General Hospital! I didn't particularly like the attention, nor did I like the fact that some people associated the study with the 'afterlife', but I had no say in the matter.

Although before starting the study I had had reservations about the possible reaction of some of my medical colleagues, I soon came to realize that most people, including doctors, nurses, pharmacists, dieticians, physiotherapists, hospital volunteers and administration staff, were actually very interested in it. At work people often asked me how 'the project' was progressing. That isn't to say that some weren't sceptical, but many of those who were were still very curious.

As the study progressed, I was invited to give presentations on the subject, first at one of the medical educational meetings and then together with Dr Fenwick at the weekly hospital medical seminars called the Grand Rounds. I felt very nervous about both of them, but they went very well and we had lots of positive feedback. Later that year I was also invited to join the Resuscitation Committee of the hospital, where I helped with training issues.

During that time, my friends and colleagues often used to tease me about the project by humming the tune from *The Twilight Zone* when I walked onto the wards! I used to just give them a quick nudge, or gently hit them, and then smile and get on with my work. As the study progressed, a cartoon appeared in a local newspaper, the *Daily Echo*, which really amused me, and it was nice to see that people outside the hospital were also seeing the light-hearted side of things.

"No, I don't want to come in – I'm just researching out-of-body experiences for Southampton General Hospital"

This cartoon is probably my favourite. It appeared in one of the local Southampton newspapers, the *Daily Echo*, after an interview about the study.

Although I could see the funny side, in general I didn't like the attention very much. I preferred just to concentrate on completing the study. Having said that, though, the increased awareness was positive in that it enabled me to receive the many fascinating NDE cases from the public that taught me so much more about the subject.

One of the last cases that I received was from a lady whose grand-son had had an NDE. She wrote:

'John's heart had stopped … There was a lot of commotion … they were pressing on his chest and he was lifeless and blue … They put him in an ambulance and took him to hospital…

'[After he had been discharged from hospital] one day, during the course of play, he said, "Grandma, when I died, I saw a lady." He was not yet three years old. I asked my daughter if anyone had mentioned anything to John about him dying and she said, "No, absolutely not." But over the course of the next few months he continued to talk about his experience. It was all during the course of play and in a child's vocabulary.

'He said, "When I was in the doctor's car, the belt came undone and I was looking down from above." He also said, "When you die, it is not the end … a lady came to take me … There were also many others, who were getting new clothes, but not me, because I wasn't really dead. I was going to come back."'

Interestingly, John's parents noticed that he kept on drawing the same picture over and over again. As he got older, it got more complex. When asked what the balloon was, he said, 'When you die you see a bright lamp and … are connected by a cord.'

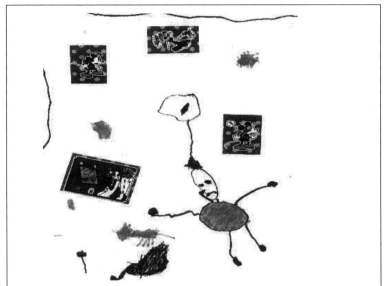

(a)

(b)

These are two drawings by John (like all other people with NDE, I have changed his name), who had the near death experience when he was under three years old. His family had at first been concerned because they saw that he kept on drawing the same theme. Here is a drawing from when he was younger (a) and one from when he had grown a little older (b).

John's case was truly fascinating and confirmed much of what I had read regarding children's NDEs.

Then a few years later I received another case which was equally captivating. The mother of the boy had written:

'My son Andrew, then three and a half years old, was admitted to hospital with a heart problem … He had to undergo open heart surgery …

'About two weeks after the surgery he started asking when he could go back to the beautiful sunny place with all the flowers and animals. I said, "We'll go to the park in a few days when you are feeling better." "No," he said, "I don't mean the park, I mean the sunny place I went to with the lady." I asked him, "What lady?" and he said, "The lady that floats." I told him I didn't know what he meant and that I must have forgotten where this sunny place was and he said, "You didn't take me there, the lady came and got me. She held my hand and we floated up … You were outside when I was having my heart mended … It was okay, the lady looked after me, the lady loves me, it wasn't scary, it was lovely. Everything was bright and colourful [but] I wanted to come back to see you." I asked him, "When you came back, were you asleep or awake or dreaming?" and he said, "I was awake, but I was up on the ceiling and when I looked down I was lying in a bed with my arms by my sides and doctors were doing something to my chest. Everything was really bright and I floated back down …"

'About a year after his operation we were watching *Children's Hospital* and a child was having heart surgery. Andrew got really excited and said, "I had that machine" [a bypass machine]. I said, "I don't think you did." He said, "Yes, I did really." "But," I said, "you were asleep when you had

your operation, so you wouldn't have seen any machines."
He said, "I know I was asleep, but I could see it when I was
looking down." I said, "If you were asleep, how could you be
looking down?" He said, "You know, I told you, when I
floated up with the lady ..."

'[One day] I showed him a photo of my mum (she had
passed away) when she was my age now, and he said, "That's
her. That's the lady."'

This is Andrew's drawing of his out of body experience. Here he is being taken by a
lady he later recognized as his deceased grandmother. (Again I have changed
Andrew's name.)

These children's NDEs were fascinating. In both cases the children had experienced an out of body state, had drawn it later and had described meeting a lady – in Andrew's case his deceased grandmother – and seeing a bright light. The content of the NDEs seemed to be simpler and the children were more limited in their ability to explain all that they had experienced, but nevertheless they seemed to have had the same core experience as adults. Children like John and Andrew surely could not have known much about the concept of death and the afterlife and hence could not have had preconceived ideas about it, yet nevertheless they recalled similar features to adults.

Obviously most of the cases that I received came from the UK and other Western countries, but I knew that NDEs had been reported in other countries and cultures too and in the years that followed I managed to interview a few people from other cultures. A middle-aged Muslim woman told me:

'I had been admitted to hospital for a major operation …
During the procedure, I found myself at the corner of the
room looking down at my body and realized that I had died …
I could see outside the operating room and the doctors were
telling my family that I had died. I felt very frustrated as I felt
comfortable at the ceiling and wanted to tell them I was fine.
There was complete peace. There was a bright warm light
everywhere. I was really distraught by the fact that my family
were so upset and they were all crying. It was very frustrating
… then the next thing I knew, I was in pain and back in my
body …'

Interestingly, when I spoke with this woman's son, he confirmed that the family had all been told that she had died.

I have since received a few other NDE cases from non-Western people and they do indeed seem to share the same core features, although to be sure of this I would really like to have performed a large study myself.

As my colleagues became more aware of my interest in the study of the human mind at the end of life, some of them started telling me more about their own experiences. One day I was on call with Dr Richard Mansfield, an experienced cardiologist who was very meticulous and serious at work. I respected him very much. That evening we had taken a break for coffee and got talking about my study. Suddenly he said:

'I don't know much about these experiences, but I can tell you something that happened to me that really freaked me out. I still cannot explain how it happened …

    'One night when I was on call there was a cardiac arrest call and together with the rest of the team I ran to the arrest. The patient was a 32-year-old man. On my arrival, he had no pulse, wasn't breathing and was in asystole [a flatline].[1] We continued to resuscitate him, even though the outcome looked bleak. We had intubated him and he was receiving oxygen, as well as having regular three-minute cycles of chest compressions and adrenaline. He had also had atropine, but despite this he remained in asystole and did not have a pulse. We carried on for over half an hour, but then started to lose all hope as he had remained pulseless and in asystole

---

1 There are generally three types of cardiac arrest: one in which the heart has a relatively normal electrical activity but still doesn't beat; one in which there is a very abnormal electrical activity, which is what stops the heart from beating; and one in which there is no electrical activity at all. This is commonly called a flatline, or in medical terms an asystole. This is the worst type and only a very small percentage of those who have this type of cardiac arrest survive. Shock treatment is only useful for those whose hearts have an abnormal rhythm and is not used in asystole.

throughout this time. Because he was young we decided to carry on, but eventually it became obvious that we were not winning and so as team leader I made the decision to stop. I checked with everyone else on the team and we all decided that it was time. Before stopping, I once more checked that the monitor and the connections were working appropriately and that the patient had no pulse. We then stopped and accepted that he was unfortunately dead. We were all very sad, as he was so young.

'I left the patient in the room with the nurses who were preparing him for his family's arrival. I went outside and sat down by the nurses' station and started writing in the medical records. As I was writing, I realized I couldn't remember exactly how many vials of adrenaline we had given him, so about 15 minutes later I went back into the room to check. While I was there I looked across at the patient and noticed that he wasn't quite as blue as when I had left him. He looked pinker, which was very strange. I looked at him again. He definitely looked pinker. Rather hesitantly I moved over and checked his groin for a pulse. I couldn't believe it! Now he had a pulse! I couldn't understand how, but he definitely had a pulse. So we had to restart resuscitation and call the rest of the cardiac arrest team back. We eventually managed to stabilize him and then transferred him to the intensive care unit.

'A week or so later he came back to the ward. To my amazement, not only had he recovered fully but he hadn't suffered any brain damage. After the arrest, everyone was sure that he would have had brain damage because not only had he been through a prolonged resuscitation while he was in asystole but also he had been left for 15 minutes afterwards without any kind of CPR [massaging of the heart] or oxygen.

'When I saw him later he told me that he had watched everything from above and described all that had happened in detail. He told me everything that I had said and done, such as checking the pulse, deciding to stop resuscitation, going out of the room, coming back later, looking across at him, going over and rechecking his pulse and then restarting the resuscitation. He got all the details right, which was impossible because not only had he been in asystole and had no pulse throughout the arrest, but he wasn't even being resuscitated for about 15 minutes afterwards. What he told me really freaked me out and to this day I haven't told anyone because I just can't explain it ... I also know that I definitely checked the monitor, the leads, the gain [this is a technical means of checking that the flatline is truly flat] and the connections as well as the pulse before stopping. I just can't explain it and I don't think about it anymore.'

I was absolutely stunned by this story. First because I really knew and trusted Richard – not only was he a highly competent cardiologist but also a very good doctor all round. If I had heard this story from anybody else I probably wouldn't have believed it. Second, I knew that he had no interest in NDEs whatsoever. Third, I knew what happened in a cardiac arrest and so I appreciated why he had been so shocked. As doctors we generally try to limit the duration of cardiac arrest, because at best we can only achieve around 30 per cent of the circulation despite all efforts. The longer this process goes on without the heart starting, the more the brain is starved of oxygen and glucose because of the relatively inadequate circulation. Therefore there is always a great risk of permanent brain damage with resuscitation, which increases as it becomes prolonged. We often face a dilemma: do we try and restart the heart at any cost and then have a patient who is left with permanent brain damage, or do we stop?

It is a very difficult decision to make sometimes. For this man not to have developed brain damage and then to have come back and recalled all the details of his resuscitation went against everything that we would have expected medically.

Soon afterwards I came across another very interesting case recalled by a doctor working with acutely ill patients. One evening I had been invited to a dinner party, where I met Joan La Rovere, an American doctor who had been working in London at Great Ormond Street Children's Hospital. She had trained in paediatrics at Harvard Medical School and then moved to the UK to further her experience at this very prestigious children's hospital. She was now working in the intensive care unit. After dinner the conversation turned to my study and surprisingly she started telling me about a child whom she had cared for a few years earlier:

'At that time I was part of a team which would go to smaller peripheral hospitals and collect sick children who needed to be at Great Ormond Street Hospital for specialist treatment. One evening I had gone with the rest of the team to a hospital in Kent, about 20 miles away from London, to collect a nine-year-old child with severe kidney failure. She was very ill and needed urgent transfer to our hospital to be managed on our paediatric intensive care unit.

'During the ambulance journey we got stuck in the rush-hour traffic and even though we were going as fast as we could with the emergency lights and sirens blazing, we could not travel fast enough. The girl's condition deteriorated and suddenly her heart stopped beating and she had a cardiac arrest. We started resuscitating her straightaway in the ambulance, but the traffic really wasn't helping. We tried over and over again and just couldn't start her heart again.

'Eventually one of the nurses said, "Look, she is dead –
why don't we drive off the main road and go to a local
hospital and have her pronounced dead?"

'Something in me said we should carry on, even though it
looked as though we really had lost her. I said, "No, we will
carry on with the resuscitation. If she is going to be
pronounced dead, it will be at Great Ormond Street and
nowhere else." So we carried on with the resuscitation.
I didn't have much hope, but something told me to start
talking to her during the resuscitation. I don't know why,
but I did it, even though it made no sense to me really.
Nevertheless, I kept comforting her and telling her not to
worry and that she was going to be okay.

'Miraculously, we got her heart restarted almost as we
arrived at Great Ormond Street. Although she was still in a
very critical and unstable condition, I was pleased because we
had managed to restart her heart and at least we had got her
to Great Ormond Street.

'At that time my job was to collect patients from other
hospitals and so I never looked after her while she was in
hospital, but I heard from the nurses that she gradually
improved and eventually was discharged home.

'One day, many months later, she came back to the
hospital to see everybody who had cared for her. During her
visit she asked one of the nurses, "Where is the American
doctor who looked after me in the ambulance and who was
talking to me during the trip?" She had watched everything
from above and had recalled all the details. I was amazed
when I heard this, as she had never even seen me throughout
the trip. She had been too ill and had been on a life support
machine ...'

Now my search for answers was getting even more interesting. It was incredible that so many highly respected doctors working with acutely ill patients had had their own experiences with NDEs. There really was something amazing going on … How could people recall details so clearly when essentially they had gone through clinical death for 30–45 minutes? This was a real quandary that could not be accounted for easily with our current scientific concepts. I couldn't even say that maybe the doctors had been wrong, because they were all very experienced and competent and very familiar with cardiac arrest resuscitation. Like Professor Chamberlain, Richard Mansfield and Joan La Rovere, I could not explain what had happened at all. I turned my attention back to our study and hoped this would reveal the answers.

At that time I used to finish work mostly around 6 p.m. My routine was then to visit the wards and follow up on any cardiac arrest patients. One day on my way home I stopped by ward D2E, the acute admissions ward, on a routine follow-up of a cardiac arrest call and approached one of the nurses to find out if the patient had survived.

'The gentleman in bed 6 had a cardiac arrest two nights ago and survived,' she said. 'I think he is by his bed now.'

I walked into the bay and followed the bed numbers with my eyes. 'Ah, number 6.' I glanced down to find a stocky middle-aged man sitting up in bed. As I approached him, he looked up at me and shuffled himself up the bed.

Pointing to my name badge, I introduced myself: 'I am Dr Parnia. I normally work on the medical unit of the hospital, although I have to tell you that I am not one of the doctors looking after you this time. I am here because I am conducting a study into the experiences people have when they are in a deep coma. I understand you suffered a cardiac arrest a few days ago and I wanted to find out if you would be willing to participate in a study.'

He looked at me in a bemused fashion and then said, 'Yes.'

As was routine, I explained the study in more detail and then got him to sign a consent form to participate in it.

'Thank you for signing the consent form. Now I really wanted to ask if you had any memories of the period when you were in a coma?'

To my surprise, for the first time I didn't get the 'Of course not, I was in a coma' look. This time the patient looked at me in a slightly guarded fashion, but didn't say anything. I sensed hesitation, so I carried on talking ...

'It is for a scientific study – you see, some people have reported having an experience when they have been in a coma and we are very interested in finding out more about what they experience. Do you have any memories from the period when you were in cardiac arrest a few days ago?'

'Yes,' he said.

I was really taken aback by this reply! I almost had to pinch myself. I had waited months for this.

'What did you experience?' I asked eagerly.

Rather hesitantly, he started to speak. 'I saw a tunnel at the corner of the room, with a bright light all over ... I felt very peaceful and calm ... During this I saw my mother who had passed away.'

All this time he was looking at me as if to say, 'Well, can I trust you?'

'Is there anything else, perhaps?' I said.

'No, that's it. I don't remember anything else.'

'You didn't have any other sensations or memories?'

'No.'

He obviously hadn't had an out of body experience, otherwise he would have told me, I thought. I didn't ask him about it anymore, as I didn't want to put words into his mouth. Even so, at last we had our first NDE case! It wasn't the breakthrough I had hoped for, but it was something. In fact it had a relatively low score of 8 on the Greyson scale. More importantly, the patient hadn't claimed to have detached from the body or watched events from the ceiling, so we couldn't ask him anything about the boards.

In the next few months we collected three other cases that did not quite fit our Greyson criteria for an NDE. Two of these were experiences that simply didn't score highly enough on the Greyson scale (as they did not include at least four NDE features) and one was completely different from an NDE. This last person described a totally bizarre experience in which he had seen some people jumping off a mountain. The other two described near death-like experiences – one had experienced seeing a light and feeling peaceful and the other had felt peaceful and seen a tunnel – but they scored less than 7 on the Greyson scale, which was not enough to classify them as NDEs.

However, during this time we also collected three cases of people whose experiences did score highly enough to be classified as NDEs. The first two had the same familiar theme of feeling peaceful and seeing deceased relatives, a bright light and a tunnel. The final case was that of a woman who was really hesitant to talk to us. All the others had also been hesitant initially, but she was really quite concerned about what people, in particular her husband, would think if they knew about her experience. Although obviously all the cases were anonymous and we were going to keep them confidential, she made us promise that nobody else would find out about it. Eventually, after a few days, she decided she could tell us what she had experienced:

'I don't know what happened, but I just felt at peace and in the distance in the corner of the room I saw a frame – it looked like a doorframe – and my father, who died many years ago, was standing there. I felt bemused at what was happening and started to go towards him. He then looked at me and put his hand out, as if to say "Stop." He told me I had to go back. I felt that if I went beyond that frame, I could not come back again ... I don't recall anything else about the experience.'

We now had four people who had described having an NDE during cardiac arrest, although none of them had described an out of body experience and so none of the boards that we had so painstakingly mounted on the ceiling and that I had changed and cleaned so regularly had been tested.

We had planned to keep this study a small pilot and, if successful, to use it as a means to expand to a large multi-centre study across the country. So, at the end of the one-year period we decided to stop and analyse the data we had already obtained before moving on to the larger study.

Analysing the Results

This had been a fairly small one-year prospective study of cardiac arrest survivors carried out on the emergency, medical and coronary care units of our hospital to analyse what people experience when they reach the point of death. It had also been the first ever study that had aimed to investigate all three theories put forward for the causation of near death experiences. It had primarily been designed with the intention of developing an appropriate method to study near death experiences during cardiac arrest. The fact that we had people describing NDE during cardiac arrest was very significant.

Before we had started the study, I had read in the medical literature that NDEs might occur in as many as 30 per cent of cardiac arrest survivors. Now this sort of figure seemed to be a gross overestimate. It was becoming very clear that although NDEs did occur in cardiac arrest survivors, the frequency of the experience, and that of out of body experiences, was far lower than people had estimated.

Over the next six months I analysed the data from our study by dividing the cases into two groups based upon whether or not people had had an NDE. All the survivors who had not had an NDE were placed into the first or control group and all those who had had an NDE were placed into the second or study group. The plan was to compare the two groups for differences that might have contributed to the causation of the experience.

I first analysed all the data regarding the brain-based theories by comparing the average oxygen, carbon dioxide, sodium and potassium levels (*Table 1*), as well the drugs that had been administered during cardiac arrest. There was no evidence to support the role of drugs, lack of oxygen, excess carbon dioxide or potassium or sodium in causing NDE. Interestingly, if anything the oxygen levels were higher in patients with NDE than those without, but we had to be very careful in interpreting this, as we had a very small sample of people with NDE compared to those without. We really needed larger numbers, but although small, our sample didn't seem to support the concept that NDEs were being caused by a lack of oxygen to the brain.

We then compared the religious backgrounds of those with NDE and analysed whether these had contributed in any way to the experience. All four people who had had an NDE were non-practising Christians – one had become a practising pagan 10 years earlier – but there were no features specific to Christianity in the experiences and they all followed the core experiences as described by Moody. There was also no obvious difference between the experience of the person who was a pagan and the others.

We had been unable to test the transcendental theories as no one had claimed to have been out of body.

The actual frequency of NDE was around 6 per cent (4 out of 63) of cardiac arrest survivors if we did not include the 2 people who had had NDE-like features but scored too low on the Greyson scale, and around 10 per cent (6 out of 63) if we did include them.

Table 1

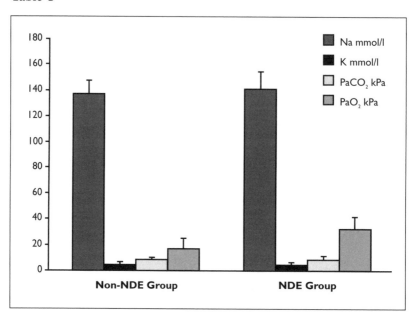

These results looking at sodium (Na), potassium (K), carbon dioxide (CO_2) and oxygen (O_2) were obtained from our pilot study. The only difference between the NDE and the control group was that the average oxygen levels were higher in the NDE group, but as there were only four patients in this group, it was not possible to be sure whether this was a real finding. For this a larger sample would be needed.

This study had been effective as a pilot in telling us how frequently NDE occurred and had also provided some data on the potential roles of brain-based and psychological theories regarding the causation of NDE, but it had been too small to answer all the questions that we had set out to address.

The study had also raised a very important question: how could people with cardiac arrest have lucid, well-structured thought processes with reasoning and memory? This seemed a real scientific paradox. I realized I needed to study what happened to the brain during cardiac arrest in more detail.

What Happens to the Brain during Cardiac Arrest?

I became more and more interested in understanding how the body actually responded to the shock of the heart stopping. After all, dying is a continuous biological process that is initially reversible, but with time becomes completely irreversible. This is why we as doctors quickly try to intervene and reverse the process through various resuscitation methods. Therefore any experience that people have during a cardiac arrest and hence during the dying process must be studied in the context of the biological changes that are taking place inside the body at that time.

The instinct to stay alive is universal. It is in fact one of the most elementary instincts that all creatures have, from the smallest ant to the largest elephant. Most living beings also have a language through which they communicate. Cells in the body are no exception to this. The difference between human language and that of cells is that rather than using sound, cells release different chemicals. So, just as we may shout or scream when under stress, cells will respond to stressful events by releasing particular chemicals. It is by coming to know these chemicals that we can learn the language of the different cells in the body and hence study them as well as the illnesses that arise from them.

For the brain, the effect of the heart stopping, and hence stopping the flow of blood to the rest of the body, is utterly catastrophic. Having studied the processes that take place in the brain and being familiar with how cells respond, I could see that for brain cells, the loss of blood flow would be comparable to a massive disaster suddenly striking a large city made up of millions of inhabitants that until a few moments earlier had all been working harmoniously together. I thought of the panic that would strike the people living in the city. At that point everything would become a matter of survival. Perhaps brain cells too try to survive, to preserve the life of the brain.

Brain cells are completely dependent for their survival on the flow of oxygen and nutrients via the bloodstream. When this stops, they start to suffer almost immediately. Brain oxygen stores and consciousness are lost within 20 seconds, after which glucose and high-energy stores are also lost. So, within a few seconds of the heart stopping, the brain cells turn to special stored energy sources, called ATP, to keep themselves alive. However, due to a very high need for energy, these stores are used up very quickly, typically within about five minutes, and then the brain cells are left without any source of energy and begin to starve. Unlike humans, who in a disaster may live for days without food, brain cells need food almost straightaway.

The shock of a lack of oxygen to the brain, which typically takes only 10–20 seconds, causes the brain cells to release a particular chemical transmitter called glutamate, which normally has the function of stimulating other brain cells. There is therefore a mass release of this chemical across the brain by the cells, which become 'over-excited' as a result. This becomes harmful to the cells and is in fact called 'excitotoxicity'. This is because the mass release of glutamate causes the cells to swell up excessively, thus causing the membrane that holds their structure together to become damaged and the contents of the cells to leak out. At the same time, the membrane holding the cells together also becomes damaged through another mechanism, as the lack of oxygen causes it to be broken down into tiny fat molecules.

However, despite all these efforts, the brain cells gradually become irreversibly damaged and eventually die. Research by doctors has shown that brain cells start to become damaged within minutes of a loss of blood flow and that if normal blood flow is not restored within about 15–20 minutes brain cell loss becomes quite extensive. During this whole period, the cells 'scream' by releasing certain chemicals and attempt to activate certain genes before losing function completely.

Numerous studies have demonstrated that immediately after cardiac arrest blood pressure drops to unrecordable levels – in most studies less than 15 mmHg, a level not compatible with life.[2] The body has special internal blood pressure receptors, and as soon as it recognizes that there is a loss of blood pressure and blood flow, it tries to raise the blood pressure and blood flow to the brain by releasing several hormones, such as epinephrine, into the bloodstream. These are the same hormones that are released during a critical illness, but as cardiac arrest is the most critical of all illnesses, the levels of these hormones are correspondingly much higher at that time. A cardiac arrest is in fact associated with the highest epinephrine levels ever recorded – 1,000 times higher than the amounts normally found in the bloodstream. As well as epinephrine, the hormones released include

---

2 Blood pressure is vital for life. In order for the body's vital organs such as the kidneys and the brain to receive nutrients, 'pressure' is needed to push blood into these organs and allow the nutrients to get into them. If the pressure drops below a certain level then the organs don't receive the nutrients. Although there is some variation, normal blood pressure is around 120/80 mmHg. The higher value (systolic) is the pressure immediately after the heart contracts. The lower value (diastolic) is the value after the heart relaxes. If the higher value is less than 80–90 mmHg, this is very worrying. It often takes place in patients who are in clinical shock. Sometimes the mean arterial pressure (MAP), a figure in between the higher and lower values, is used. Under normal circumstances this is around 80–100 mmHg. Doctors will often become concerned if the MAP is less than about 60–70 mmHg, as levels below this may hinder blood flow to the vital organs, including the brain. Obviously, if the blood flow to the vital organs drops sufficiently, then the organs stop functioning. For the brain, the first signs are confusion and drowsiness, followed eventually by coma.

norepinephrine and vasopressin. All of these are extremely potent at increasing blood pressure, so potent in fact that they have been developed for medical purposes and are now given to patients who have very low blood pressure or have had a cardiac arrest. These hormones cause the blood vessels in the body to tighten up and hence squeeze blood up towards the brain. They also act on the heart and try to stimulate it into action, but unless the heart beats, they have almost no effect.

In addition to these hormones, many other hormones are released, such as prolactin, endorphins, the body's own morphine-like substance, and β-lipotropin, all of which have the function of ameliorating the adverse effects of a lack of blood pressure.

Despite all these efforts by the body itself, however, once the heart stops, breathing stops and within a few seconds brain cells become damaged, stop functioning together and eventually die, unless doctors start to interfere with this process and attempt to restart the heart.

WHAT HAPPENS DURING MEDICAL RESUSCITATION?

Although modern heart and lung resuscitation, which is now commonly known as cardiopulmonary resuscitation, or CPR, was established in the 1950s and 1960s, historically various other methods had been used to try and bring someone back to life. Early resuscitation attempts involved heating the body, using warm ash and hot water, whipping, blowing hot smoke in the mouth and rectum, and rolling people back and forth on a wine barrel or a horse to help the chest expand and take air in.

Since the 1960s resuscitation methods have continued to develop through international collaboration and research, but the basic techniques have remained the same and involve compressions of the chest wall to help push blood around the body and also the placing of a tube in the windpipe to allow oxygen to be delivered to the lungs. Unfortunately, though, cardiac arrest still carries a very high rate of death.

Studies have shown that chest compressions are not capable of producing adequate blood flow to the brain, due to a combination of inadequate blood pressure being generated and an increase in the pressure inside the brain itself, which means that even higher blood pressure is needed to push blood up into the brain. It has also been shown that due to various physiological processes that take place during cardiac arrest, blood flow to the brain remains quite low even if the actual measured blood pressure generated during compression seems reasonable.

During conventional CPR, without the use of stimulating drugs such as epinephrine, brain blood flow has been found to be less than 5 per cent of normal values. The addition of drugs such as epinephrine can in some circumstances increase brain blood flow to 30 per cent of normal levels. However, I realized that even with resuscitation, there was still significantly reduced blood flow to the brain, to levels that were not compatible with brain cell electrical activity. Research had shown that after resuscitation had been commenced, the mean arterial pressure had risen marginally to approximately 30–40 mmHg, but had still remained well below the levels needed to adequately enable blood to flow to the brain. In fact the blood pressure had only returned to a level high enough to allow adequate blood flow to the brain after the heart had finally been restarted. I recalled that while I had been training we had been taught that during resuscitation at best we could only restore 30 per cent of the output of the heart. Now I could see why – we could not raise the blood pressure to a high enough level. Obviously, the inadequate blood flow was also the reason why there was always a concern that there could be brain damage during cardiac arrest.

In some studies brain function had also been monitored using an electroencephalogram (EEG) (*see Figure opposite*). This is a device that measures electrical activity arising from the surface sections of the brain (cortex) where higher brain functions, such as sound, vision, sensory input, thought processes and memory are mediated. In the first few seconds after the heart had stopped and hence the blood pressure had dropped, the EEG waves changed to an initial slow phase and then quickly to a 'flatline'. This 'flattening' of the EEG waves indicated a lack of measurable electrical activity in the brain. This took on average 10 seconds to develop from the time that the heart had stopped. The EEG remained flat during the entire cardiac arrest resuscitation, which corresponded with the period of inadequate blood pressure and hence inadequate blood flow to the brain that had been recorded in the other studies. It was only after the heartbeat had been restored that the EEG began to show some activity.

If there was a delay in starting the resuscitation, the brain waves not only remained flat during the resuscitation, but also for almost two hours after the heart had been restarted. This is because the brain cells had been starved of oxygen and in response had released many chemicals which had had the effect of constricting or narrowing the blood vessels that carried blood to the brain. Therefore it had taken a few hours for the vessels to open up sufficiently to allow blood to flow and to lead to electrical activity in the brain.

The EEG measured activity on the surface of the brain, but other studies had demonstrated that when the surface area of the brain (cortex) stopped functioning, as measured with the EEG, there was also no activity in the deeper structures, including the brain stem, the area at the base of the brain that keeps us alive.

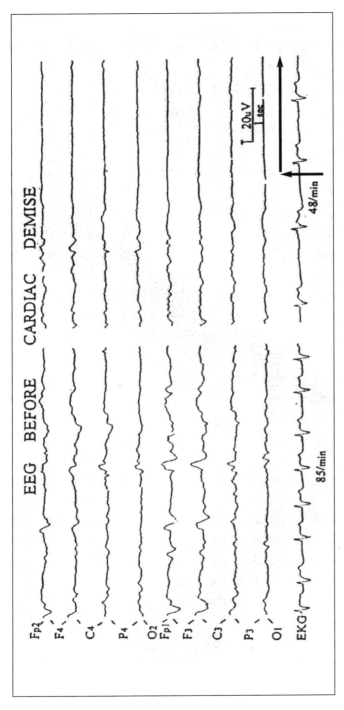

The EEG is a means of measuring the electrical activity taking place in the brain and in particular the cortex of the brain. Many studies have shown that during a cardiac arrest when there is severe reduction in blood flow to the brain, the EEG waves go flat and remain flat throughout. This may actually happen even before someone's heart has completely stopped. It is an indicator of a lack of adequate blood flow. In the case shown here, the patient's heart stopped, but the EEG actually went flat (*arrow*) when the blood pressure dropped to around 40 mmHg and the heart was still beating at 48/min. From then on it remained flat throughout the cardiac arrest.

The Paradox

I got thinking about the implications of this. *There is something that just doesn't fit here*, I thought. *Here we have a group of people who are so severely ill that they have reached the clinical point of death, yet somehow they report having lucid, well-structured thought processes, together with reasoning and memory formation from that time. There are also reliable anecdotes of patients who have recalled detailed events that have taken place during resuscitation. How can this happen? How can there be such clear and lucid thought processes when the brain is at best severely disrupted and as far as we can measure not functioning?*

That was particularly intriguing. Normally people who are very ill develop an acute confusional state, which is characterized by confused and disordered thought processes together with memory loss. That is understandable because when the delicate balance of nutrients, hormones and other essential substances around the brain becomes disrupted then of course it cannot work properly. The vast majority of people from our study had complete memory loss for the period of cardiac arrest, which is what I would have expected, but 6–10 per cent paradoxically seemed to have thought processes and consciousness, in other words an NDE. Even though they also lost memory of the events surrounding their illness, they remembered the NDE very clearly.

There were four possible explanations. The first was that maybe the experiences had not taken place during the cardiac arrest, even though people genuinely believed they had. Memory is fallible, so perhaps they had taken place during a very short period of time either before or after the brain had stopped functioning.

However, although this was certainly a possibility, it couldn't apply to the cases where people had recalled watching events that had occurred in the middle of the cardiac arrest and had been verified by medical and nursing staff. For this to have happened, there must have been consciousness present at a time when all the scientific studies had demonstrated at best a severely disordered brain and at worst no brain function at all.

Also, it didn't entirely fit with our current knowledge of how the brain responds to a severe insult such as a head injury or a severe lack of oxygen. Any kind of insult to the brain leads to a period of memory loss just before and after the event. In fact memory is a very sensitive indicator of brain injury and the length of memory loss is a good way of determining the severity of the injury. Events that occur just prior to loss of consciousness would not be expected to be recalled and recovery following a cerebral insult is confusional – just like the man who had written to me about his NDE after an accident and had said, 'I do not have any recollection of my condition or the events that happened in hospital … but I do recall quite clearly an experience that is very hard to put into words ...' It just didn't make sense for people to remember the NDE so clearly and nothing else.

The second possibility was that perhaps our measurement of brain function was not sensitive enough. Perhaps there was activity in the brain during a cardiac arrest, but we just couldn't measure it using an EEG. As time goes on, however, and we develop more accurate means of measuring the function of the body, perhaps we will be able to gain a clearer picture.

This still didn't seem to be adequate, however. Thought processes are mediated by multiple areas of the brain. So even if there were some minute activity in the individual cells that we couldn't measure, this would still be unlikely to lead to adequate electricity being generated for the brain cells to communicate with each other.

Another possibility was that perhaps consciousness and thought processes were not mediated by brain cell electrical activity after all. Perhaps a different mechanism was involved. Although this seemed counterintuitive at the time, I later found out that some scientists had begun to explore the possibility of subatomic quantum processes mediating consciousness.

The fourth possibility that had to be considered was whether consciousness functioned even when the brain did not. This idea was of course not compatible with mainstream scientific views regarding the relationship between the mind and the brain, but objectively speaking it had to be examined, as we simply didn't know what type of matter mind and consciousness were, how they came to exist and what their relationship was with the brain.

Our study had been too small and obviously much more research was needed to understand exactly what was happening, but nevertheless we had answered some questions and another interesting question had now been raised. Together we finalized the text and the paper was accepted for publication in the medical journal *Resuscitation*.

At this time we also started to prepare for a much larger study that we hoped would provide definitive data regarding the outcome of the human mind at the end of life. We would use the experiences gained from our pilot study to examine the occurrence of NDEs in over 1,000 cardiac arrest survivors.

Other NDE Studies

One day out of the blue I received an e-mail from Dr Pim Van Lommel, a cardiologist from Holland. I didn't know him, but he said that he had also performed a study of NDEs in cardiac arrest and he very kindly sent me a copy of his research.

I got very excited. This had been a much larger study than ours. The aim had been to investigate the occurrence of NDEs in cardiac arrest patients and also the factors that affected the frequency, depth and content of the experience. The researchers had followed 344 cardiac arrest survivors from ten hospitals over a two-year period and 41, or 12 per cent, had reported a core NDE. The researchers had found that the occurrence of NDE was not associated with duration of cardiac arrest, unconsciousness, medication or fear of death. Patients had then been followed for a further eight years and had been found to have undergone a transformational change in personality. Those who had had an NDE showed a significant difference in their social and religious attitudes as well as their attitudes towards death. They had more involvement in the family, empathy and understanding of others, less fear of death and a more spiritual outlook on life.

This study confirmed that NDEs lead to a transformational change that is greater than the result of simply coming close to death. The authors of the Dutch study also concluded that since all cardiac arrest survivors underwent the same biological changes and were given the same drugs during cardiac arrest, NDEs were unlikely to occur as a consequence of these factors, since if they were, then most people with cardiac arrest would have an NDE.

A very interesting finding was that during the study approximately 24 per cent of those who had an NDE also had an out of body experience. In one case, a nurse had reported that during a cardiac arrest she had removed the patient's dentures and placed them in a drawer in a special trolley. The resuscitation had been protracted and had gone on for one and a half hours. Throughout that time the man had remained in a coma. Afterwards he had been transferred to the intensive care unit. One week later he had returned to the same ward where the nurse worked. He had apparently seen her and said, 'Oh, that nurse knows where my dentures are.' He had then gone on to say, 'Yes, you were there when I was brought into hospital and you took my dentures out of my mouth and put them into that car [meaning the crash trolley]. It had all these bottles on it and there was this sliding drawer underneath and that's where you put my teeth.' The nurse had said:

'I was especially amazed because I remembered this happening while the man was in a deep coma and in the process of CPR. When asked further, it appeared that he had seen himself lying in bed and that he had perceived from above how the nurses and doctors had been busy with CPR. He had also been able to describe correctly and in detail the small room in which he had been resuscitated as well as the appearance of those present … At the time … he had been very much afraid that we would have to stop CPR and that he would die. And it is true that we had been very negative about his prognosis due to his very poor medical condition when admitted.'

In the following year a third study of NDEs in cardiac arrest was completed in the US, by Professor Bruce Greyson. He had followed up 1,595 people who had been admitted to hospital with heart disease over 30 months. Of these, 7 per cent, or approximately 110 people, had had a cardiac arrest and 10 per cent of those had had an NDE. Those who had had an NDE were not different from those who had not in terms of social or demographic variables, cognitive function or degree of heart disease. This study had not directly tested the mechanism of causation of NDE.

Soon afterwards, a fourth study investigating NDEs in cardiac arrest was completed by Janet Schwaninger, a cardiac nurse who had worked in the US. In this study 23 per cent of cardiac arrest survivors had an NDE and six months later they had been transformed in a positive manner.

These other three studies were very informative as they confirmed that NDEs occurred in 10–23 per cent of cardiac arrest survivors. They also confirmed that the experience had a transformational effect and that out of body experiences had been reported. Unfortunately none of the researchers had directly tested the theories for the causation of NDEs or the validity of the out of body claims.

The authors of these other studies had, however, raised questions regarding the mechanism of causation of NDE in cardiac arrest.

Professor Greyson had concluded by saying:

> 'The paradoxical occurrence of heightened awareness and
> logical thought processes, without subsequent amnesia, during
> a period of impaired cerebral perfusion [blood flow to brain]
> raises particularly perplexing questions for our current
> understanding of consciousness and its relation to brain
> function.'

It was very interesting that we now had four independent studies of NDEs in cardiac arrest and all four had raised the same questions regarding the mechanism of causation of NDE and the relationship between the mind and the brain. How could thought processes, memory formation and reasoning be occurring at a time when there was little or no brain function?

These studies further re-inforced our commitment to set up the largest ever study of NDEs during cardiac arrest. Perhaps the answers were within reach now. In the meantime, maybe we needed to re-evaluate our views about the relationship between the mind and the brain, the possible nature of consciousness and even the nature of reality itself.

5

Understanding Mind, Brain and Consciousness

Most people look at the brain in awe, and rightly so. Just the sight of it is immensely awe-inspiring. I remember the first time I saw someone's brain during an operation to remove a blood clot. I was working on the neurosurgical unit at Southampton General and we had admitted a lady called Sheila to the ward. Sheila was in her late fifties and had presented to hospital with a stroke following an internal bleed. She needed an urgent operation in the middle of the night as the clot was pressing against the brain, causing brain damage. I was assisting the neurosurgeon, Dr Carter. During the operation he removed a small area covering the brain and behind the clot I saw a pinkish grey organ pulsating with every heartbeat. It was a phenomenal feeling.

I had seen many operations before, but there was something really special about watching the brain. Its beating created an almost hypnotic state in me. I felt a sense of seduction, fascination and awe. I wondered whether it was this feeling that had captured the hearts and minds of people like Dr Carter and driven them to become neurosurgeons. As I watched this small grey organ pulsating in front of me, I thought to myself, *Here lies Sheila – her memories, feelings, emotions, love for her husband and children, her free will, her conscience, her sense of right and wrong, her intuition … All that is Sheila is lying in front of me in this pulsatile organ. Isn't it?*

Inadvertently, that night I had entered into a fascinating debate on perhaps the greatest mystery facing science today: the nature of consciousness and the mind. The basic scientific problem was simple to describe but difficult to answer: how did Sheila's unique awareness, thoughts, feelings and emotions arise from her brain? Traditionally in philosophical circles this has been referred to as 'the mind-body problem' and although it has been a focus of philosophical debate for millennia, scientists have only really become interested in it in recent times.

As I stood there watching the surgeon performing the operation on Sheila's brain, I thought for a moment about the problem of consciousness. How could the little grey cells that made up the brain I was watching also produce thoughts and feelings? How did they give rise to the unique subjective inner world that we all experience during our daily lives?

I started a mental tour of the brain and its component parts. Like many other complex structures in the body, I knew the brain was made up of a number of different parts, all connected in a way which allowed it to perform its overall function.

The brain has two mirror-image halves, called the cerebral hemispheres, which, according to one brain scientist, Professor Ramachandran, resembles a 'walnut sitting on top of a stalk, called the brain stem'. Each half of the mirror-imaged brain, or hemisphere, is divided into four areas that have different functions: the frontal, parietal, occipital and temporal lobes, which make up the surface structure of the brain called the cortex. There are also some areas that lie between the stalk and the cortex, including the areas responsible for the initiation and modulation of movement, temperature regulation and goal-directed behaviour such as eating, drinking and reproduction, together with the expression of emotions. These sections are also connected via tracts of nerves to the rest of the brain and the rest of the body.

During the surgery I was watching the area called the cerebral cortex, the structure on the surface of the brain that is involved with higher brain function, including thought processes, listening, seeing, counting, drawing, recalling memories and moving particular muscles such as the arms and legs. I knew that the frontal areas were concerned with some very mysterious aspects of the human mind and human behaviour such as moral sense, wisdom, ambition and other activities of the mind about which we know very little. Damage to the frontal section of this part of the brain typically causes changes in personality and problems with the sensation of touch as well as with speaking, whereas damage a little further behind, in the parietal area, can cause problems with speech as well as the use of arms and legs. These areas are also concerned with creating a three-dimensional representation of the spatial layout of the external world, and of our own body within that three-dimensional representation.

Further back is the occipital area, which is involved with vision and damage to which can result in blindness, and to the side is the temporal region, which is involved with certain aspects of memory, hearing, emotions and visual perception.

Underneath the cortex or main surface structure of the brain, which mediates all higher brain functions, is the stem, otherwise known as the brain stem, which maintains all of life's vital processes, including heartbeat and breathing, as well as important reflexes such as the pupillary reflex, which controls the size of our pupils in response to light, and the gag reflex, which prevents food and other swallowed objects going down the windpipe. The other important function of the brain stem is maintaining wakefulness. So damage to the brain stem may lead to unconsciousness, loss of vital reflexes and eventually death.

Due to its position the brain stem is also very much like a highway junction through which all the connections between the body and brain pass. For example, all the nerves carrying sensations from the rest of the body converge in the spinal cord before travelling up through the brain stem and then branching off to the different sections of the brain, including the cerebral cortex, where the higher functions are carried out. Messages are then relayed back to the body from the cerebral cortex via the brain stem.

Behind and just above the brain stem lies the area of the brain that is responsible for the regulation and co-ordination of our movements such as walking and running. This is the third main structure in the brain and is called the cerebellum (*see Figure opposite*).

Sheila had developed a blood clot that was pressing against the middle or parietal area of the surface of her brain and so she had developed weakness of her arms and legs. The aim of the surgery was to relieve this pressure and restore power to her arms and legs. In Sheila's case we also had to operate to remove the blood clot because sometimes a large blood clot above the brain surface can push down so much against the brain that it can compress the brain stem and cause damage and can even be fatal.

Looking at Sheila's brain, I remembered how the different areas of the brain were in a constant state of communication through electricity carried by long tracts of nerves. Although I could not see it, I knew that there were continuous flashes of electricity going right along the brain as well as coming up from the deeper structures to the surface and vice versa. If any area of the brain became damaged, this would affect the normal patterns of electricity, which is why an EEG monitor, which measures electricity, can be used to diagnose brain diseases.

The source of the electricity flowing across the brain was special-ized brain cells called neurones. I knew that the brain was thought to be made up of 100 billion of these neurones and that they formed the

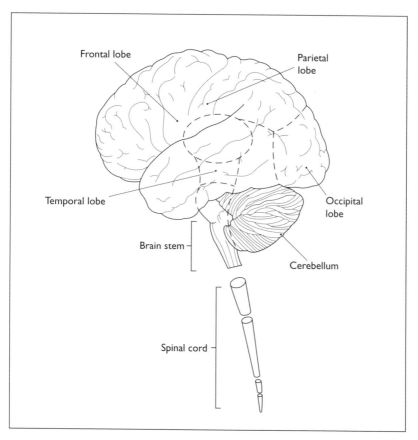

Frontal lobe

Parietal lobe

Temporal lobe

Occipital lobe

Brain stem

Cerebellum

Spinal cord

This diagram illustrates some of the different sections of the brain. The larger white structure, like a walnut, is composed of the different sections relating to higher brain functions. Impulses from the five senses arrive through the nerves at the spinal cord or the section above it, the brain stem, and then travel up to the cortex. Messages are then sent back to the rest of the body from the cortex and other sections of the brain via the brain stem and the spinal cord. The bud-like structure with more black and white lines is the cerebellum and is responsible for balance.

basic structure and functional units of the nervous system. Each neurone is connected to other brain cells through 1,000 to 10,000 contacts called synapses. It is here that exchange of information takes place between brain cells. This is incredible – with around 100 billion cells, each with 1,000 to 10,000 connections to other cells, the total number of permutations and combinations of brain connections and hence activity is almost infinite! All the different brain states, including all our emotions, such as love, hate and anger, as well as our thoughts, ambitions and even religious sentiments, are mediated by these connections or synapses, which have themselves been shown to vary and become more complex if a certain area of the brain is being used and developed. In fact it is thought that no two people, even twins, will have exactly the same brain connections or wiring, since these synapses or connections develop and change constantly according to different stimulation of the brain areas during our lifetime. This is because as we grow, learn and generate new experiences, the connections in our brains become more extensive. These ultimately depend, then, on the richness of experiences.

The neurones themselves are constantly generating electricity through the passage of positively and negatively charged chemical elements, such as sodium, in and out of the cells via special gates on the surface of the cells. The electricity then flows along the entire length of a cell until it reaches another brain cell. At that point it causes a special chemical, called a neurotransmitter, to be released from the first cell onto the next cell, where it causes gates on the surface of the second cell to open, which again generates the electricity along the length of that cell by allowing positive and negative elements to go in and out of the cell. Sometimes when these neurotransmitters are released, they have the effect of stopping the electricity from going along any further at the next junction and at other times they may cause further action at the next nerve junction. This is how they stop a signal or send it on.

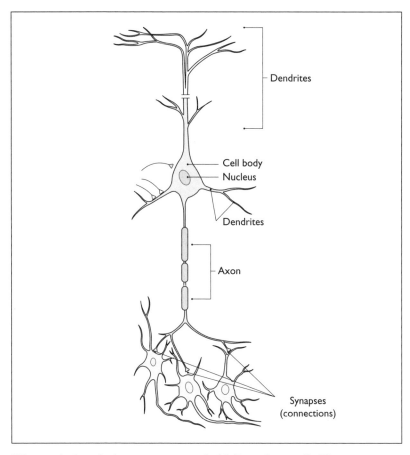

Dendrites

Cell body
Nucleus

Dendrites

Axon

Synapses
(connections)

When we look at the brain it is composed of different brain cells. The one involved with sending electrical impulses is the neurone. Here it can be seen how one neurone connects with many other cells. Each neurone is like many other cells and is composed of a 'body' within which lies the 'nucleus'. This contains all the genes and codes for the production of many protein-like chemicals that mediate the effects of the cells. These include chemicals such as neurotransmitters. The cell also has many arms with fingers at the end (dendrites) that stretch out and connect with similar arms coming off other brain cells, thus forming a network of cells. Each cell also has a long arm that sends a signal along, called an axon.

Each network of cells, which may be made up of many millions of cells, mediates a specific function or different functions of the brain, such as the conscious sensation of 'seeing'. Each of the connections, which is similar to two people holding hands, is called a synapse. A synapse is like a railway junction through which an arriving impulse, just like an arriving train, is either sent on its way or stopped. This depends on the chemical (neurotransmitter) that is released. Some are inhibitory (like a red light), while others are excitatory (like a green light). It is at the level of the synapses in the brain that some scientists, such as Professor Susan Greenfield, have proposed that 'consciousness' may arise.

Like almost all other cells in the body, neurones also produce proteins and protein-derived chemicals in response to a special code. This code is essentially in the form of genes that are in the nucleus, or control room, of each cell. The chemical products sometimes have the function of maintaining the structure of the cells themselves and at other times may be released from the cells to have an effect on neighbouring cells.

As well as neurones there are also other cells, called glial cells, in the brain which do not produce electricity but just act as support for the electricity-producing neurones. Their name comes from the Greek for 'glue', because when looked at through a microscope some of these cells appear to be attached to the neurones like glue. They are like scaffolding maintaining the structure of the brain while the wire-like neurones transmit the messages.

The brain is thus a highly complex and well-organized mesh of electrical wires that form a network of electrical superhighways conducting information to and from the most distant parts of the body. So in the brain it is not an individual cell that performs a particular function, rather a large group of cells all connected together, otherwise known as a 'neural network'. It is therefore the overall activity of multiple areas of the brain that is involved with all the functions of the brain, including conscious experiences such as thoughts, vision and hearing.

Thoughts and the Brain

Science has largely got to grips with the mechanisms that lead to various signals and messages being transmitted in the brain and the connections between the brain and the rest of the body. But where in the midst of all this electrical activity and chemical processes do thoughts lie? How does the passage of electricity across a cell lead to feelings? When I take a bite from an apple, scientifically we can track all the pathways from my tongue to the cortex of the brain that mediates this taste, but how do these chemical and electrical processes turn into sweet and sour?

This is the problem that has baffled philosophers, psychologists and scientists throughout the ages. David Chalmers, an Australian philosopher, has summarized it very well: 'Consciousness poses the most baffling problems in the science of the mind. There is nothing that we know more intimately than conscious experience, but there is nothing that is harder to explain.' In his books he has called this the 'hard problem' of consciousness. This is in contrast to the 'easy problems', which essentially involve understanding the mechanisms that allow the brain to deal with the various sets of information that it receives. These are the processes that we have largely discovered.

Modern medicine has helped answer some of the questions regarding the relationship between thoughts and the brain, namely the specific areas that are involved with certain feelings, emotions and thoughts, but not the question of how thoughts are actually produced from brain cells.

Modern methods of analysing thought processes now involve special brain scanners called functional MRI (magnetic resonance imaging) and PET (positron emission tomography) scanners. These work upon the principle that brain cells have a constant need for blood, which carries with it all the vital nutritional substances that they need to work, including oxygen and glucose. So the scanners essentially detect and follow the movement of blood to various parts of the brain. This way they can tell us which part of the brain is working more actively at any time.

I thought of how farmers in dry areas of the world such as Egypt form canals to carry water from a main river to the areas of land that they are cultivating. In the brain there is a very similar system in operation. Instead of a single river such as the Nile, there are two main vessels that carry blood to the brain. Then there are smaller vessels that act as canals carrying blood to other areas. Sometimes

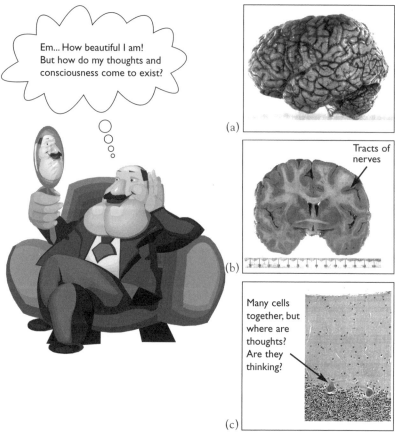

Em... How beautiful I am! But how do my thoughts and consciousness come to exist?

(a)

Tracts of nerves

(b)

Many cells together, but where are thoughts? Are they thinking?

(c)

Even though we have come to understand the structure of the brain and the cells that make up the brain, the biggest question in science today is, how does electricity travelling down the arms of the cells and across the junctions lead to the amazing phenomena of thoughts, conscious feelings, emotions and sensations? When this man looks at himself in the mirror and admires himself, how do these thoughts and feelings arise?

This problem is better understood when we examine a real brain (a). Here we see the surface or cortex; then, looking at it through a section (b), we see the tracts running up to the cortex. These are made up of millions of the axons, or arms, arising from millions of neurones all bundled together to form the tracts of nerves that we can see. In another section (c) we see a cell body itself with the many projections or arms around it.

The big question is, how do thoughts arise from this cell? If I were to look at this cell and someone were to tell me it was thinking *I feel guilty, or hungry,* I would probably think that person was a little bit mad. Yet if a single cell can't think, how can many of these single cells attached together through electricity and chemicals produce thoughts? If I throw a brick at my neighbour's window, should these cells feel 'guilty'? How does free will arise from these cells, or is everything just predetermined?

farmers around the Nile increase the flow of water through a particular canal to cultivate a specific area of land. Then they may change the flow so that more water gets to another area. Now if, using satellite technology, I could observe the changes in the flow of water through the canals from space, I would be able to tell which parts of the land were being worked on at any one time simply by observing the changes in the flow of water in that region. In a similar way, brain scanners detect changes in the flow of blood to various regions of the brain.

In addition to detecting changes in blood flow, specialized scanners can also detect the areas of the brain that have increased their consumption of oxygen and glucose. So by following the changes in flow of blood and the consumption of oxygen and glucose (metabolism) to various parts of the brain scientists can understand which areas of the brain are involved with certain thought processes. This is called 'mapping' the brain. To do this, scientists will place someone into a scanner and scan the brain while they are having certain thoughts.

As I read what I have written, changes are constantly taking place in the flow of blood to certain parts of my brain. I am also enjoying music and this pleasant feeling is accompanied by a reciprocal change in the pattern of blood flow to the part of my brain involved with this sensation. If I really get into my music and stop paying attention to the screen, the areas that had been receiving more blood while I was reading will now receive less blood, but other areas will then start to receive more blood. Interestingly, brain scans have shown that for any thought many areas of the brain become active and that it is therefore multiple areas of the brain that mediate thought processes. This is a very important point.

However, identifying blood flow changes or increased metabolism of certain parts of the brain during an experience doesn't answer the big problem, which is: how does a physical collection of cells give rise to conscious experience?

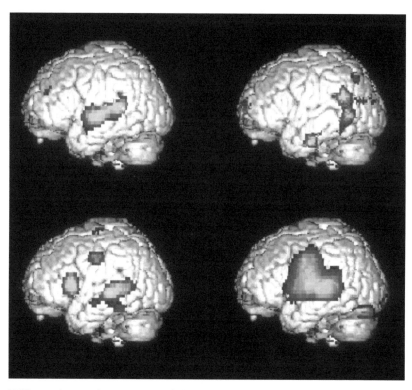

PET scan showing brain activity while speaking/listening. Here we can see how different groups of cells may become active with a specific conscious process. This doesn't, however, mean that the cells are producing thoughts or feelings, it just tells us that there is increased blood flow and glucose uptake into them.
Source: Wellcome Department of Cognitive Neurology/ Science Photo Library

Common Theories about Consciousness

In the months after the conclusion of our study, I started examining the literature to study the views of scientists on the problem of consciousness and the mind. I knew that the answer to the significance of our study and the other studies of near death experiences in cardiac arrest lay in understanding the nature of consciousness.

While many well-known philosophers such as Plato and Descartes had argued that the mind and brain were separate entities, many but by no means all modern scientists had proposed that the mind and consciousness were somehow products of brain activity. Unfortunately, however, despite obvious interest in this area, nobody had yet been able to propose a plausible biological mechanism to account for how the brain might give rise to the mind or consciousness. The problem was that no one even seemed to know how to start thinking about it scientifically. There was no obviously conceivable way that consciousness could arise from the currently understood mechanisms in the brain. This had led many scientists to believe that this mystery might never be solved by science.

One method of studying this area that had been introduced by scientists in the last 15–20 years had been to determine the brain-based changes that take place under certain conditions and to correlate them with conscious experience. In other words, scientists had attempted to study the biological processes that take place in the brain when someone has a conscious experience, such as seeing an object or thinking. These had been called 'the neural correlates of consciousness' (NCC).

When studying these, many scientists had pointed out that it was important to remember that just because something correlated with something else, it didn't necessarily mean that it caused it. This is a basic law of studying correlations in any field of science. When any correlation is observed between two events, there are three possible explanations. Let's take the example of two actions, A and B. If there is a correlation, then either A is causing B or B is causing A or some other process is causing both of them. So when correlations are found between brain-based events and conscious experiences, all of the possibilities must be considered. We know that brain-based events correlate with thoughts, but no one has been able to demonstrate whether A causes B or B causes A or both. In other words, perhaps the brain-based events cause conscious experience or maybe conscious experience causes the brain-based changes, or perhaps something else causes both of them.

Looking through the medical and scientific literature I found that although many views had been expressed regarding the nature of consciousness, they could essentially be divided into two groups. The first was made up of conventional brain-based theories that suggested mind and consciousness were produced from the brain. The second was comprised of theories that were considered to be 'non-conventional' and looked beyond currently understood brain processes. Although the more common scientific view had been the former, both groups included theories from leading international academics and Nobel Prize winners.

CONVENTIONAL BRAIN-BASED THEORIES OF CONSCIOUSNESS

The most commonly held view in the scientific literature was that mind and consciousness were by-products of brain activity, just as, for example, light arises from the action of electricity passing through a light bulb or heat arises from the burning of coal. Hence they were not the same as the underlying processes that take place in the brain, in the same way that light coming off a light bulb is not the same as the activities that are taking place in the light bulb.

Although, as mentioned above, experimental evidence demonstrating how this can happen is still lacking, nevertheless a number of different theories have been proposed to account for it. These theories have attempted to tackle different aspects of the problem of consciousness, such as how conscious experience may arise from brain cells, or how the different aspects of consciousness may bind together to form a single unified sense.

This is a particularly interesting and mind-boggling problem. As I sit here writing this book and drinking coffee, I am receiving numerous inputs into my brain at the same time. On the one hand I am seeing light coming off the computer screen while I watch my hands typing away and on the other hand I can taste the bittersweet taste of coffee. In the background I can see my green-coloured dressing-gown, the window, with railings outside, the table and the many other objects scattered nearby. I am also listening to the radio, to a song by Leanne Rimes, while feeling the weight of my body against the chair. All that I am experiencing at this moment is part of one conscious state, yet all these different aspects of consciousness are actually mediated by many different areas of the brain. I know that vision itself is divided up into colour, motion and form processing and mediated by 30 or so areas of the brain. Therefore when I take a simple example of conscious experience, such as what I am experiencing right now, and ponder on all that is happening, each aspect is probably being mediated by hundreds of areas of the brain simultaneously, yet remarkably I experience it all as 'one' and not hundreds of different and separate consciousnesses. This is what neuroscientists call 'the binding problem'.

Several views have been proposed to account for how conscious experience may arise and how the binding of consciousness into 'one' may occur. It has been suggested that:

1. Mental states arise from specific patterns of activity within networks of brain cell connections.
2. Synchronized and rhythmic electrical activity in networks of brain cells leads to conscious awareness and the binding of conscious experience.

3. Consciousness emerges as a novel property of computational complexity among brain cells. It has further been argued that brain cells and their chemical connections are the fundamental units of information in the brain and that conscious experience emerges when a critical level of complexity is reached in the brain's neuronal networks (the networks of brain cells).

1. The role of neuronal connections

A noted scientist with an interest in the problem of consciousness is Professor Susan Greenfield of the University of Oxford. She has proposed that the mind may arise from the activity of brain cells at the level where the cells are connected together (the synapse). Rather than arising from a single isolated region of the brain, she suggests that consciousness arises diffusely from the brain cell connections.

The reasoning, Greenfield argues, is that there is no single complete function that takes place in one region of the brain. As mentioned above, it is known, for example, that vision is divided up into many separate components that are connected together to give rise to the conscious experience of seeing, such as colour, motion and form processing, and the function of vision can preoccupy over 30 brain regions. Similarly, any one brain region can participate in more than one function. So brain regions are smaller parts of a wider brain stage and not units that work alone. Thus we know that conscious experience arises from the actions of many different parts at the same time. However, when we break each area of the brain down into its smaller constituents, we see that each area is a complex circuit which is ultimately reduced down to the connections between the cells, or synapses, or in other words, to the individual wires of the circuits themselves across which electrical signals are passed. This signalling is dependent on a series of different biological products, or proteins, which are themselves products of genes. Therefore, Professor Greenfield has proposed that the neuronal correlate and in effect the physical substrate of the 'mind' is a process that occurs at the level of the brain connections, or synapses, which are not only highly dynam-ic but also reflect experience through their strength and extension of connections. She has not been able to propose how actions at the level of the brain cell connections lead to conscious experience. Nevertheless, she also proposes that it is this process, whereby connections so exquisitely mirror what happens to us, which leads to the 'mind'.

According to this theory, consciousness, or our sense of self-aware-ness, is thought to arise from the interaction of assemblies of neurones involving up to tens of millions of neurones all connected together. It is proposed that at any one time there may be many neuronal assemblies present; however, the largest assembly will dominate and determine that moment of consciousness.

The degree to which cells are recruited and hence the degree of consciousness will be determined by a variety of factors, such as the strength of the input coming into the brain, for example from the eyes and the fingers, as well as pre-existing connections and the degree of competition, as shown by the smaller assemblies starting to form. So let's imagine we are standing on the street, holding something in one hand. An assembly of brain cells related to 'touch' is active, so we are aware of what we are holding. Then, suddenly, we see something that interests us, for example an accident. We then stop feeling what we are holding and just experience what we are seeing. At that time the activity of the assembly of brain cells related to touch would be overtaken by the new assembly of cells which would have become active in relation to what we have seen. The activity of these cells is in turn determined by the activity of various proteins, which may change in response to other signals, including events that take place in our body, such as hormone changes, immune changes or changes in the levels of the neurotransmitters. So in the same scenario, if we had the 'flu and were feeling very ill, certain chemicals

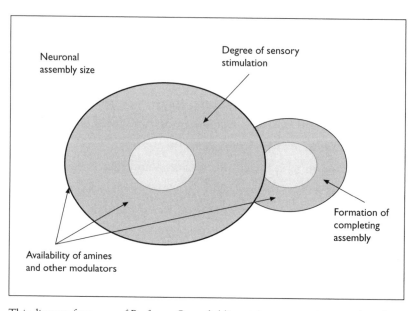

Neuronal
assembly size

Degree of sensory
stimulation

Availability of amines
and other modulators

Formation of
completing
assembly

This diagram from one of Professor Greenfield's articles on consciousness describes her view that there are always different networks of cells, as depicted using the circles. At any one time one network or assembly of cells is more strongly activated, then with the arrival of another stimulus another network may become stronger and take over. The amines are various chemical triggers that the cells release when activated. Here the larger circle shows a larger network of active brain cells. The smaller circle shows another active network of cells, but only the stronger (larger) one comes in our conscious experience, even though there may be many other networks active at any one time. *Source:* Modified from Greenfield, S, Mind, brain and consciousness, *Br J Psychiatry* 2002; 181:91–3; reproduced by kind permission of The Royal College of Psychiatrists.

and hormones would be released by our body and immune cells that would also interact with the brain cell networks, so we would feel 'unwell' while seeing the interesting event.

It has thus been suggested that the subtlest influences either from outside or inside the body modulate consciousness at the level of cell synapses in the brain and hence lead to differences in consciousness and that there is always a competitive process going on between different assemblies of cells.

2. Synchronized and rhythmic electrical activity in networks of brain cells

This theory predominately aims to describe the intermediary pathway that may lead to the unified sense of self.

The late Francis Crick, a Nobel Prize winner and the co-discoverer of DNA, and Christof Koch of the California Institute of Technology have proposed that a starting point for the study of consciousness is the study of the correlates of visual consciousness, in other words the changes in brain-based biological processes when we are conscious of seeing things. Crick and Koch have argued that all the different aspects of consciousness (for example, pain, visual awareness, self-consciousness) may employ a basic common mechanism or perhaps a few such mechanisms. Hence understanding and discovering the mechanism for one aspect may allow an under-standing of the other aspects too.

Although Crick and Koch accept that it is difficult to account for how conscious experience arises from the activity of the brain, they propose that there must be some specific underlying differences in brain cell activity that lead to the phenomenon of consciousness. Thus they propose that in order to study visual consciousness it is important to identify the brain-based biological events that take place during visual consciousness and correlate them. It is hoped that these will ultimately help identify the specific mechanisms that lead to the phenomenon of visual awareness. Crick and Koch have observed that brain cells responsive to shape, colour and movement may become active in synchrony in the general range of 40 times per minute (40 Hertz). They suggest that synchronized activation of brain cells in this range (roughly 40 times per minute, but perhaps as low as 35 and possibly as high as 75 times) might be how the brain puts together visual consciousness.

Furthermore, as an area of the brain called the thalamus appears to play a central role in mediating consciousness, and conscious experience also depends on the surface of the brain or the cortex, they suggest that consciousness may depend on synchronized firing in the range of 40 Hertz in the networks of cells connecting the thalamus and the cortex. This is sometimes called '40-Hertz oscillation'.

So, basically it is thought that this rhythmic and synchronized activity of neurones may be the neural correlate of awareness and might serve to bind together activity concerning the same object in different brain areas. At present, however, there is little experimental evidence to support this suggestion directly and it still does not account for how either the actual process of consciousness or the binding of consciousness arises.

3. Consciousness as a property of neuronal computational complexity

Daniel Dennett, an American philosopher and author on consciousness based at Tufts University, has expressed perhaps one of the most reductionist and materialistic views regarding consciousness, which at first glance even he acknowledges appears counterintuitive!

In his view there are no such things as subjective experiences, instead he proposes that the brain is like a computer that has inputs from different sources with a disposition to a particular behaviour and an ability to discriminate between different stimuli. He believes that much of what we learn is acquired simply through social imitation. So he has proposed that consciousness is essentially created through the global activity of brain circuits, which create a virtual 'captain of the crew' or 'self' that ultimately governs the overall functioning of the brain, but that the whole process is very much like a very complex computer that acts according to a program, without any 'real' subjective experience. It is all a complex system of inputs and outputs and modulation of information with no actual subjective experience.

Dennett has proposed that at any given time many modular cerebral networks (in other words, specialist networks of brain cells) are active in parallel and process information in an unconscious manner. A piece of information then becomes conscious if the brain cell population that represents it is mobilized by competitive, co-operative and collateral activities into a brain-scale state of activity that involves many neurones distributed throughout the brain. Dennett postulates that this global availability of information is what we subjectively experience as a conscious state.

OTHER BRAIN-BASED THEORIES OF CONSCIOUSNESS

Many other theories have been put forward to account for the potential neural correlates of consciousness. A German neuro-scientist, Hans Flohr, has argued that consciousness is dependent on a specific receptor in the brain called the NMDA receptor. This is a receptor on which many anaesthetics act, and as they can temporarily take away consciousness, Flohr has therefore concluded that the normal functioning of this receptor is required for consciousness. However, other researchers have argued against this, saying that there are other anaesthetic drugs that do not act on this receptor. In addition, this receptor is also involved in other brain processes as well, including unconscious states.

Gerald Edelman and Giulio Tononi from the Neurosciences Institute in San Diego in the United States have proposed a biological theory of consciousness in which it is suggested that consciousness may arise from the interaction of two parts of the brain. They propose that a key mechanism underlying conscious experience is the interaction between an area that is involved in perceptual categorization and another area related to memory, value and planning for action. It is thought that such interactions among groups of brain cells in different brain areas may be necessary in order to generate a unified brain-based process corresponding to a conscious scene.

In addition to the areas proposed in these theories, many other areas of the brain have been proposed to be the potential neural correlates of consciousness. However, although they were very interesting, all these theories seemed more or less to share the same limitations.

SOME LIMITATIONS WITH THE CONVENTIONAL BRAIN-BASED THEORIES

In general, evidence to back up the concept that mind and consciousness arise from the brain has come from the clinical observation that specific changes in function such as personality or memory are associated with specific areas of damage to the brain, such as those that occur after head injury or a stroke. This finding has been further supported by the results of studies using functional MRI and PET scanning, in which, as described above, specific areas of the brain have been shown to become active in response to a thought or feeling. However, although these studies provide evidence for the role of neuronal networks as an intermediary for the manifestation of thoughts, they do not necessarily imply that those cells also produce the thoughts.

In fact many scientists have argued that brain-based theories cannot fully explain the observed features of consciousness. The limitations of the conventional theories can be divided into four broad categories, which are examined below.

1. The nature of subjective experience

The most obvious limitation of such theories is that they do not provide a plausible mechanism that may account for the development of consciousness from brain cell activity. The theories simply propose potential intermediary pathways that may be mediating consciousness but do not answer the fundamental question of how subjective experiences may arise from the activity of neurones. This is a point that has been summarized very well by Professor Greenfield. She concludes: '... just how the bump and grind of the neurones and the shrinking and expanding of assemblies actually translate into subjective experience – is, of course, another story completely.'

2. The binding of spatially distributed brain activities into unitary objects such as consciousness

How do brain activities that are distributed within multiple areas of the brain bind into a unitary sense, such as occurs with vision, or the development of a coherent sense of self? In other words, how do we go from multiple inputs from millions of brain cells to a single picture or a single sensation of the self?

3. Transition from pre-conscious processes to consciousness itself

The theories proposed do not account for how an event that is pre-conscious (in other words chemical or electrical events that are not 'conscious' as we know it) becomes conscious, other than to say that it 'somehow' occurs at a critical point.

4. Free will

A fundamental part of our lives involves the notion of free will. We are judged in society based upon our intentions and actions and the brain-based views expressed above cannot account for this. If correct, they would mean that our lives would be completely determined by our genes and environment and hence there would be no place for personal accountability. Can you imagine the situation that would arise if everyone claimed that everything they did was due to the action of their genes in combination with their environment? No one could really be held accountable any more! Thankfully, society still runs with the notion of free will and personal accountability.

These and other limitations with the conventional views have led some scientists to seek alternative explanations for consciousness.

NON-CONVENTIONAL THEORIES

Quantum processes

Stuart Hameroff, an anaesthetist at the University of Arizona, and Roger Penrose, a mathematician from the University of Cambridge, have raised many of the limitations of the theories above. In particular they argue that these theories cannot fully explain the observed features of consciousness.

The quantum processes theory put forward by Hameroff and Penrose is based upon the principle that there are two levels of explanation in physics: the familiar classical level used to describe large-scale objects and the quantum level used to describe very small events at the subatomic level.

At the quantum level superimposed states are possible, that is, two possibilities may exist for any event at the same time, but at the classical level either one or the other must exist. So, for example, we can either go right or left, but not both. When we make an observation, we are working at the classical level, so although there may be subatomic processes going on at any one time, with the potential of different superimposed states, when we make an observation, the superposed states have to collapse into one.

Hameroff and Penrose propose that consciousness arises from tiny tube-like structures made of proteins that exist in all the cells in the body, including brain cells, and act as a skeleton that allows cells to keep their shape. They propose that these small structures are the site of quantum processes in the brain, due to their structure and shape. They argue that consciousness is thus not a product of direct brain cell to brain cell activity, but rather the action of subatomic processes occurring in the brain.

In support of their theory, they further argue that there are single-celled organisms such as amoebae that, despite lacking brain cells or synapses, have consciousness and are able to swim, find food, learn and multiply through their microtubules. Hence they suggest this may be a more advanced structure leading to consciousness.

So Hameroff and Penrose propose that consciousness may arise from subatomic quantum processes occurring in the protein structures that make up the microtubules. They argue that these tube-like structures undergo switching between two or more states, due to the action of weak chemical attraction forces, a process that takes place within nanoseconds. It is thought that the microtubule conformational changes could support classical information processing, transmission and learning within neurones. Therefore Hameroff and Penrose argue that owing to these processes at any one time there may be a number of different quantum states or possibilities and when a decision is made it is the result of the collapse of one state, which then reaches consciousness. This is called the Orchestral Objective Reduction (Orch OR) theory.

Other Non-Conventional Views

Some have, however, argued against the Orch OR theory by pointing out that microtubules exist in cells throughout the body and not just in the brain. Also there are drugs that can damage the structure of microtubules but appear to have no effect on consciousness. More importantly, it has been argued that although the Orch OR theory may potentially account for how the brain carries out complex mathematical problems, it still fails to answer the fundamental question of how subjective experiences and thought processes arise.

This limitation of all the theories mentioned above has led to the suggestion that consciousness may in fact be an irreducible scientific entity in its own right, similar to many of the concepts in physics, such as mass and gravity, which are also irreducible entities. The investigation into consciousness has thus been proposed to be similar to the discovery of electromagnetic phenomena in the nineteenth century or quantum mechanics in the twentieth century, both of which were inexplicable in terms of previously known principles.

Some, such as David Chalmers, have argued that this new irreducible scientific entity is a product of the brain, whereas others have argued that it is an entirely separate entity that is not produced by the brain.

The late Sir John Eccles, a neuroscientist who won the Nobel Prize for medicine in 1963 for his work on brain cell connections and was considered by many to be one of the greatest neuroscientists in the world, was perhaps the most distinguished scientist who argued in favour of such a separation between mind, consciousness and the brain. He argued that the unity of conscious experience was provided by the mind and not by the neural machinery of the brain. His view was that the mind itself played an active role in selecting and integrating brain cell activity and moulded it into a unified whole. He considered it a mistake to think that the brain did everything and that conscious experiences were simply a reflection of brain activities, which he described as a common philosophical view:

'If that were so, our conscious selves would be no more than passive spectators of the performances carried out by the neuronal machinery of the brain. Our beliefs that we can really make decisions and that we have some control over our actions would be nothing but illusions.'

He further argued that there was 'a combination of two things or entities: our brains on the one hand and our conscious selves on the other'. He thought of the brain as an 'instrument that provides the conscious self or person with the lines of communication from and to the external world, and it does this by receiving information through the immense sensory system of the millions of nerve fibres that fire impulses to the brain, where it is processed into coded patterns of information that we read out from moment to moment in deriving all our experiences – our perceptions, thoughts, ideas and memories'.

According to Eccles,

'We as experiencing persons do not slavishly accept all that is provided for us by our instrument, the neuronal machine of our sensory system and the brain, we select from all that is given according to interest and attention and we modify the actions of the brain, through "the self" for example, by initiating some willed movement.'

Eccles' theory was well described in his book *The Self and Its Brain*. However, he acknowledged that he was still unable to explain how the mind carried out these activities and how it interacted with a separate brain. This is a point on which he was criticized by others.

In a number of books and numerous lectures held at the Sorbonne in Paris, Bahram Elahi, a professor of surgery and anatomy with an interest in consciousness, has expressed the view that although the mind and the brain are separate, nevertheless the mind or consciousness is not immaterial. Rather, it is composed of a very subtle type of matter that, although still undiscovered, is similar in concept to electromagnetic waves, which are capable of carrying sound and pictures and are governed by precise laws, axioms and theorems.

Therefore, in Elahi's view, everything to do with this entity should be regarded as a separate undiscovered scientific discipline and studied in the same objective manner as other scientific disciplines. He argues that as science is a systematic and experimental method of obtaining knowledge of a given domain of reality, then 'consciousness' can and should also be studied with the same objectivity. Each scientific discipline such as chemistry, biology and physics has its own laws, theorems and axioms, and in the same manner 'consciousness' should also be studied in the context of its own laws, theorems and axioms. In his view, consciousness is also a scientific entity and a type of matter, however it is a substance that is too subtle to be measured using the scientific tools available today. Therefore in his view the brain is an instrument that relays information to and from both the internal and external world, but 'consciousness' is a separate subtle scientific entity that interacts directly with it.

This seemed to me to be a very different way to tackle the problem of consciousness. Essentially what Eccles and Elahi seemed to be saying was that consciousness was a separate entity from the brain, interacting with it but not necessarily produced by it. This view, largely a dualist view, was more in line with the views of philosophers such as Descartes rather than those of most modern scientists; however, in view of the lack of plausible biological mechanisms to account for consciousness being a product of brain cell activity, it had to be considered.

I knew from the history of science that scientists had often been confronted with problems that had been unsolvable when examined using the scientific principles of the time. For example, when the British scientist James C. Maxwell first discovered electromagnetic phenomena in the nineteenth century, electromagnetism had to be described as a scientific entity in its own right, as it could not be explained according to known scientific principles. It was many years later that the first radio waves (which are electromagnetic waves) were recorded by the German scientist Heinrich Hertz and now we have a whole area of science that is based upon them, not to mention numerous devices such as radio, television, microwaves and infrared cameras. Maybe consciousness, too, was not reducible in terms of currently understood mechanisms of brain cell activity and its true nature would only be discovered when our science progressed further, but the major point for study now was whether or not consciousness was produced by the brain or could be a separate entity.

At the end of my study of the literature on the nature of consciousness, I came to the conclusion that we would have to accept either the broad view that mind and consciousness are by-products of brain cell activity or the view that they form a separate undiscovered entity. Either way, we didn't seem to have the scientific tools to measure mind or consciousness, so a way was needed to study them and their relationship with the brain indirectly. Until now there had been no way to test any of these theories experimentally. Perhaps studying the state of the human mind during cardiac arrest would help unravel the mystery. This seemed to be the only time when we could study the state of the human mind at a time when circulation to the brain had shut down to a point where there was no recordable electrical activity in the brain centres. Yet if consciousness truly continued and could be demonstrated objectively, as many had claimed, surely this would be a very significant discovery regarding the nature of consciousness and the state of the human mind at the end of life.

6

The Ingredients of Life

As I thought about the nature of consciousness, I thought back to an experience that I had had a few years back during a research trip to Sweden. One day my hosts had taken me out to the countryside to show me Swedish country life. That morning we all baked a very delicious flat Swedish bread. I enjoyed it very much and the memory of that day still lives on in my mind.

Although at first glance it may appear that baking bread has nothing to do with the nature of consciousness, that day, from just a few simple ingredients, we had made something tasty and delicious. Come to think of it, it wasn't just bread that was made of simpler ingredients – everything that we use and interact with in our daily lives and the world beyond is made up of simple ingredients too. This includes the food we eat, the objects we use, our homes, and of course all living beings, including ourselves.

I had to think back to basic principles. We exist within the wider universe and so does our consciousness. Although science is not yet able to measure consciousness, undoubtedly it does exist and is therefore confined within the realms of physics and matter. Therefore it should be bound by the same universal laws that govern all other beings and matter, just as we ourselves are.

I thought about the ingredients that make me what I am. Basically, I am a collection of billions of cells, which are themselves composed of numerous molecules. These cells communicate with each other through other molecules and the end result is an incredibly precise yet complex machine that is unrivalled. But even the molecules in my body are themselves made up of different combinations of atoms and the atoms themselves are also made up of simpler constituents. We now know, through the science of quantum physics, that everything in the universe is made up of basic particles of matter.

Of course the idea that all beings are made of more fundamental structures is nothing new. It actually dates back to Ancient Greece. The philosopher Democritus was arguably the first to put forward the idea of atoms. However, it was the nineteenth-century British scientist John Dalton who formally advocated that everything was made from tiny atoms. Later on scientists not only accepted that atoms existed but also discovered that some atoms shared similar chemical properties. This discovery allowed atoms to be categorized into groups, known as the periodic table. It also indicated that atoms themselves must be made up of simpler building blocks. It was the simpler building blocks in different combinations that determined the specific chemical properties of the atoms.

At the turn of the twentieth century scientists went on to discover that the atom had a small dense nucleus, made of protons, which had a positive charge, and neutrons, which had no charge. As the century progressed it was discovered that negatively charged particles called electrons were in constant motion around the nucleus and that the protons and neutrons which made up the nucleus were composed of even smaller particles, called quarks. The majority of the atom is actually made up of the nucleus.

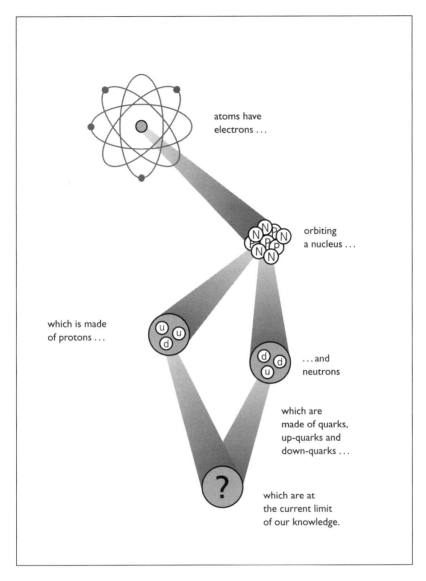

atoms have
electrons . . .

orbiting
a nucleus . . .

which is made
of protons . . .

. . . and
neutrons

which are
made of quarks,
up-quarks and
down-quarks . . .

which are at
the current limit
of our knowledge.

Although at school I was taught that everything is made up of atoms, I came to realize that atoms themselves are made up of fundamental subatomic particles. These are called quarks and leptons and when combined together make up 'larger particles', eventually atoms and then molecules. The fundamental particles sometimes behave like waves and sometimes like particles and are connected through vast distances at speeds greater than the speed of light. Here we see that the atom is made up of a nucleus that is itself made up of neutrons and protons (these are made up of the more fundamental particles, the quarks) and also electrons. *Source:* www.particleadventure.com

Throughout the 1950s and 1960s, physicists raced forward in their attempts to discover the particles that made the building blocks of the atoms and hence the universe, and numerous particles were discovered. Later, in the 1970s, scientists formulated the Standard Model, in which the large number of particles was explained as different combinations of a relatively small number of fundamental particles. This model describes all matter and the interactions between them and now, using it, physicists are able to explain what the universe is composed of and what holds it together.

All the known matter particles are composites of a number of fundamental particles called quarks and leptons. Quarks exist in groups with other quarks and thus make up composite particles, which in turn make up larger particles. There are a total of six quarks and six leptons. The electron is the main lepton, although others also exist. So everything, from the smallest atom to molecules, cells, animals, humans, mountains, planets and galaxies, is made from these fundamental particles – everything, including me, with my sense of self and consciousness, sitting here questioning the whole thing, asking why and how!

We also know that objects and matter in general interact with each other, sometimes across great distances. Just think of the effects planets have on each other, or how the moon and the sun make the waters in our rivers and seas rise up and down, or how magnets attract or repel without touching. There are therefore invisible forces in the universe that can act at different distances without touching each other.

How do forces interact 'invisibly' across such distances? Scientists have discovered that all the forces in the world can be attributed to just four interactions. These are called gravitational interaction, electromagnetic interaction and 'weak' and 'strong' interactions. They affect matter of different nature and across different distances. Gravitational interaction affects particles with mass and governs the large-scale structure of the universe because of its infinite range. Electromagnetic interaction affects particles with charge. It too has an infinite range, but is much stronger than gravity. The other two forces act at very short ranges at the subatomic level. Strong interaction affects the particles that are made from quarks, whereas weak interaction affects all particles. It is, as its name suggests, very weak and its range is extremely short.

So even though I had always thought of a 'force' as something that just happened, I realized that according to physics at a fundamental level, a force isn't an event that just happens between particles, it is itself also due to the exchange of other particles, called 'force carrier particles'. Force carrier particles are thus a group of particles that carry different forces between other particles such as quarks. In the case of light or radio waves, which are part of the electromagnetic spectrum, the force carrier particles are known as 'photons' and can travel at the speed of light. Although the force carrier particle for gravity hasn't yet been discovered, it is thought to exist, and has been named 'graviton'. The exchange particles that act between quarks and mediate the strong force are called 'gluons'. So, ultimately, all beings and all interactions take place through just a few basic particles.

Looking back through the years and observing how scientific progress has taken place, it became clear to me that at some time in the future it may be discovered that quarks and electrons may not be fundamental after all and are themselves made up of other particles. However, as far as we know today, quarks are like points in geometry. They are the fundamental building blocks of the universe. And even if there are more fundamental building blocks, the concept remains the same: the entire universe is made up of combinations of elementary subatomic particles.

WAVE-PARTICLE DUALITY

A very interesting discovery which took place in the twentieth century was that light, which is a wave, also has the properties of particles in certain situations. When light travels, for example, it behaves like a wave, but when it arrives at a surface it behaves like a particle. So it was discovered that light could be both wave and particle.

It was then proposed that if waves could sometimes behave like particles, perhaps the reverse could also be true. Experiments carried out by Louis de Broglie, and then independently confirmed by others, demonstrated this to be the case. So it was shown that other matter is also like light. Thus matter can exhibit the properties of both waves and particles. So the fundamental building blocks which combine to build up all living things are essentially a type of matter that can act like a particle at times and a wave at other times.

QUANTUM AND NON-LOCALITY

According to discoveries made by quantum physics there is also a phenomenon known as 'non-locality', or action at a distance, where particles can act on each other across great distances and at a speed even greater than light. To many people this has profound implications, as it means that many events may be interconnected and may also suggest that even the mind or consciousness can act in a 'non-local' manner.

Like many others who have studied these concepts, I was really intrigued by the potential implications of the findings that have been made in the subatomic world. It was so interesting that things can behave so differently when studied at a very small level and that sometimes their behaviour may even appear to be opposite to our own concepts of how things should be.

I could not help but wonder what role these processes could play in consciousness and the human mind.

THE POSSIBLE NATURE OF CONSCIOUSNESS

Since everything else in the universe is made up of combinations of subatomic particles, then consciousness must also be made up of these particles. They combine to form different types of matter, some of which we can perceive with our senses and others which we cannot. So, in order to answer the big question about how consciousness arises, I realized that we as researchers need to maintain a completely open mind.

It is obvious that there is much more to the world than what we can perceive with our senses. All we have to do is turn on our TV or radio or use a mobile phone and this becomes obvious to us. Our senses are like tools with which we can understand the world beyond; however, like any tool, their range of function is necessarily limited. Our eyes and the circuitry that connects them to the brain can detect light waves, for example, and then decode these in the brain as images of the world outside. But light is simply one of the waves that make up the electromagnetic spectrum (see Table 6.1). There are also others such as radio waves, infrared rays, X-rays and microwaves. We can't detect these waves, simply because they are at a frequency that our eyes are unable to pick up. The human eye can only detect electromagnetic waves with a wavelength that lies between 400 millionth of a centimetre and 700 millionth of a centimetre.

When a wavelength gets longer than this, it is called infrared. Although we are incapable of seeing in this range, it is thought that some snakes can. When the wavelength gets shorter, it is called ultraviolet. Again, although we are not capable of seeing in this range, bees can. We know of no animals that are capable of detecting waves either shorter than the ultraviolet range or longer than the infrared range, but we can measure and make use of these wavelengths through specific instruments, such as X-rays and CT scans, and other devices such as radios, mobile phones and TV. But at any time there is also more in the world than we can detect even

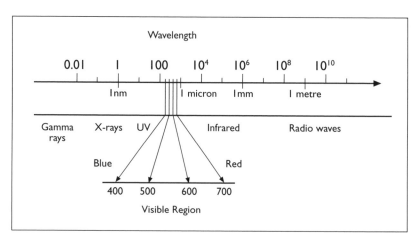

Table 6.1 Electromagnetic spectrum

with our instruments – that is why new devices and instruments are constantly being developed to help us understand more of the world around us.

Interestingly, although we cannot detect electromagnetic waves without the appropriate instruments, they are capable of conveying sounds and pictures. So these subtle waves, which are made up of very basic subatomic particles, can convey a great deal of information, including elements such as sound and vision which are part of our own consciousness. It may therefore be that a combination of fundamental particles can lead to the formation of both our physical body, with cells and organs which we can perceive with our senses, and also our consciousness and thoughts, which are of a more subtle type of matter which we are unable to measure today, simply due to a lack of instruments. In the same way that 50 years ago we were unable to 'see' in the dark whereas today we can do so using infrared cameras, undoubtedly in the future we will have instruments that can detect thoughts and consciousness.

The question that then arises is: are these thoughts and consciousness simply a product of brain cell activity and therefore only exist within the skull, or are they produced through a different mechanism and can they function beyond the brain and even become non-localized? This is where I saw a potential role for the study of human consciousness during cardiac arrest and it was here that my questions became even more intriguing.

7

Is It Real?

In September 2002 a headline appeared on the website of the American broadcaster CBS: 'Out of Body Experiences Explained'. This was in fact one of the headlines that had appeared in many of the global media outlets following the publication in the leading scientific journal *Nature* of the bizarre occurrence which happened in Switzerland to a 43-year-old patient being treated for epilepsy.

A group of Swiss doctors had carried out a procedure that is often performed on patients with intractable epilepsy. Electrodes are implanted in the brain and used to stimulate different portions of the brain. The aim is to find an abnormal brain circuit that is causing the recurrent seizures. In this case, as the doctors had been doing this, quite unexpectedly the patient had reported seeing herself 'lying in bed, from above' and also 'floating' near the ceiling. However, she had not had a full out of body experience, as she had only been able to see her legs and lower trunk.

Despite the fact that this wasn't quite like other out of body experiences that I had come across, it seemed to me that the Swiss doctors had been able to induce an out of body-like experience in someone. This seemed to suggest that the reported sensation of leaving the body during a brush with death might simply be an illusion created by abnormal stimulation of a specific area of the right side of the brain, called the angular gyrus. In fact the Swiss study had concluded that out of body and near death experiences might be influenced by a portion of the brain misfiring.

This finding had touched on one of the biggest debates since the first reports of NDEs and out of body experiences: were these experiences real or were they illusory products of normal or abnormal brain activity?

To many people the Swiss study certainly seemed to indicate that these sensations were just illusions. One psychologist, Michael Shermer, had been reported as saying, 'It's another blow against those who believe that the mind and spirit are somehow separate from the brain … In reality, all experience is derived from the brain.'

Others had been more cautious. Psychiatrist Professor Bruce Greyson of the University of Virginia, the researcher who had devised the Greyson scale, had suggested that the experiment did not necessarily prove that all out of body experiences were illusions. He had been reported as saying, 'We cannot assume from the fact that electrical stimulation of the brain can induce out of body experience-like illusions that all out of body experiences are therefore illusions.'

So what are near death and out of body experiences? Are they simply tricks of the mind or are they real?

The answers received so far had depended to some extent on who had been asked. Most of the people who have had an NDE truly believe that they have encountered the afterlife. Other people see NDEs as positive confirmation of their belief in the afterlife. Others, however, believe the experiences cannot be real, as they believe that after death everything ends. Unfortunately, for most people, their views regarding NDEs are formed by their own philosophical beliefs.

In order to be able to understand the significance of NDEs, I realized that I had to really go back a few steps and critically examine the question of how we experience the world and understand what is 'real'.

How Do We Experience Reality?

In considering the reality of NDEs, I thought more about how we gather information from the world around us. In effect the brain and the five senses that are connected to it can be likened to a very complex computer that has various sensors attached to it through which it can gather information. Yet all our senses are limited. As mentioned earlier, a bee's eye or a snake's eye can detect wavelengths which our eyes cannot. Dogs have a far more sensitive sense of smell than we have, and so we use them in our ports and airports to look for illegal substances.

Of course we are able to build various devices to help us detect things that lie outside the range of our physical senses. When I look at cells in a laboratory during the course of my work, I cannot see individual cells, yet if I use a light microscope, I can see them in detail and if I use an electron microscope, I can even see the individual structures that make up each cell. Despite this, however, I am still limited in what I can perceive.

The reason for this is that not only are all our senses limited, but so too is our brain. We can only perceive things in a three-dimensional form, but in modern times scientists have discovered that there are other dimensions beyond the 3D world. Therefore we know that our perception is limited. In effect, the brain is like a computer which allows all the information that it receives to be processed according to the limitations of the hardware and software with which it is fitted.

I recall my own reaction when I first came across an Escher picture (*see below*). This was a simple example that showed me how my brain was limited in its ability to interpret the world around me. When I followed the water pathway up, it all made sense until I reached the

M.C. Escher's Waterfall. Looking at these pictures made me realize that my own brain was limited in its ability to perceive and determine reality. (*Source:* Copyright the M.C. Escher Company-Holland. All rights reserved. www.mcescher.com)

waterfall and then it made no sense at all. Somehow my eyes and brain were limited in their ability to interpret what they were seeing! This is also true of many other so-called visual illusions. Moreover, with this simple example at least I can see my limitations, whereas with the universe beyond I may not even be aware of them.

HOW DO I SEE REALITY?

When I look at a painting, I see a picture because electromagnetic waves in the range of visible light coming off that object go through my eye and cause a chemical reaction that activates cells in the back of my brain. My brain's software then gives meaning to that activation of cells, producing a picture in my mind.

Now if someone could activate that exact area of my brain artificially, I would see that exact picture. So simply being able to reactivate a specific area of the brain that is involved with a visual experience doesn't make that sensation unreal. Identifying the mechanics of the process cannot determine whether it is real or not. It just tells us what the pathways are.

Similarly, if we were to study any particular state of mind, we could identify the specific areas of the brain that become active when that feeling is taking place. For example, if we were to place a mother inside a scanning device and then show her her giggling baby, we would be able to identify the areas of the brain involved with maternal love. Nevertheless, this would neither explain how that particular feeling arises from the brain processes nor its significance.

The same concept applies to NDEs. Many scientists have debated which parts of the brain are involved in NDEs and have theorized that they may be due to brain cell activity in the limbic or temporal lobes. What we do know is that each area of the brain processes multiple functions and that 'conscious' states such as seeing, thinking, feelings and emotions are mediated in many areas at the same time. As already mentioned, when someone is about to die, the body initially responds by releasing certain chemicals and steroids to try and maintain the blood pressure and allow sufficient blood to get to the brain. After a while, however, the blood pressure drops and there is thus reduced blood flow to the brain, which will in turn activate certain parts of the brain and lead to the near death experience. Although I acknowledge that we still do not know exactly which areas are involved, undoubtedly brain processes do mediate the experience. But the discovery of the exact areas will not explain the significance of near death experiences. Neither will it make a near death experience 'unreal' or a hallucination, in exactly the same way that discovering the areas of the brain involved in viewing pictures or experiencing maternal love doesn't make those sights or feelings hallucinations.

In fact the finding by the Swiss researchers is not new. In the 1930s the pioneering American neurosurgeon and researcher Dr Wilder Penfield used electricity to stimulate parts of the brain as part of his treatment of epilepsy. He had noted that while stimulating the temporal lobe, one of his patients had felt that she was leaving her body.

Obviously these conclusions are based upon single-case reports of out of body-like sensations following electrical stimulation of the brain and far more research is needed before definitive conclusions can be made. Also, although these isolated cases are fascinating, there have been many others where stimulation of that exact area of the brain does not induce these sensations. The Swiss doctors themselves were quite surprised by their finding, as they and other doctors who perform that particular procedure had stimulated those areas of the brain many times before. No one knows why that particular woman had that particular experience. Nevertheless, it is obvious that an area of the brain mediates out of body experiences and this could be it.

Interestingly, although out of body experiences have been reported with NDEs, they can also occur in isolation and in response to very different stimuli, including severe anxiety, pain and even deep relaxation. Therefore it may be that the same area of the brain that becomes activated during a close encounter with death can also become active in response to different stimuli.

During out of body experiences people have 'seen' events taking place and in many cases others have confirmed these details. Obviously if out of body experiences are simply illusions, then no verifiable events should be witnessed and independently confirmed. This is particularly the case with cardiac arrest patients, where there is severe impairment of brain function. So again, simply identifying the areas of the brain mediating an experience doesn't explain the meaning of that experience or indicate that it is in any way an illusion.

Therefore I realized that we cannot objectively say that the out of body experience is not real. We simply don't know. The only way to know is to conduct objective studies to answer the question and not allow our own socially formed prejudices to sway our decisions. This is particularly important for scientists studying the phenomenon. We surely need to keep an open mind and accept the results of appropriately designed studies.

I further realized that in many ways it was perhaps unwise to try and determine whether such experiences were real or not, for even determining reality is not straightforward.

WHAT IS REAL?

Studying sociology, I realized that everything that we think of as reality is not only mediated by the brain but also given meaning by society. Each culture provides guidelines as to how to view the world and in effect determines what is real.

According to sociologists, nothing contains built-in meaning and whatever meaning exists is socially determined and thus arbitrary.

We have given something meaning, but we could just as well have given it a different meaning. It is through a social process that we determine meanings: that is, people jointly decide on the meanings to assign to events and objects. Since meanings are arbitrary, people can change them, so that when circumstances change, definitions become 'outmoded', even definitions about fundamental aspects of life.

However, even when definitions no longer 'work', change does not come easily and many people will resist it. The source of any radical new ideas is extremely significant in determining whether or not they gain acceptance. If the person proposing the new ideas is authoritative, then their views will be accepted far more readily than those of someone who is perceived as being less important. Also, if an individual can drum up group support, then there exists a social basis for the new definition. Sociological experiments have demonstrated that if something is believed by enough people, others will also start to believe it. Also, if someone believes something, it is possible to make them change their mind about that 'reality' if they believe that others don't agree with it. So, if the group that offers the new definition can get enough others to accept it, the common definition of reality will change.

There is an area of sociology called social constructionism that is concerned with discovering the ways in which individuals and groups create their perceived reality. It involves looking at the ways in which social phenomena are created, institutionalized and made into trad-ition. Social construction describes subjective rather than objective reality – that is, reality as we can perceive it rather than reality as it is. True reality may actually be very different from what we perceive. For example in this room there are undoubtedly a multitude of sound waves that lie outside the frequency that my ears are capable of detecting and there are also electromagnetic waves that lie outside the range that my eyes are capable of detecting. I perceive a certain reality that is based upon what I am able to detect. If I were able to detect everything in this room, I would undoubtedly have a different perception of reality. So, reality is essentially limited to what we can perceive and to what is socially accepted.

As regards NDEs, at present, as we have seen, whether they are 'real' or not depends on the social group that we ask. If we ask those people who have had an NDE, they mostly believe that it was a real experience, whereas if we ask a group of sceptics, they will say NDEs are not real. By this they mean that there is no external reality for them.

In many ways the experience and the debate, as well as the work around it, reminded me of the work being done in the study of religious experiences.

ARE RELIGIOUS EXPERIENCES REAL?

For many who have had an NDE, the experience has had a profoundly religious effect on them, changed their outlook and led them to live more altruistic, less materialistic lives. Perhaps, I thought, in order to understand NDEs better, we needed to understand religious experiences better. Many people have in fact likened NDEs to religious experiences.

Although the scientific study of religious experience is still in its infancy, there has certainly been some progress in this area in the last 30 years. Dr Andrew Newberg, a radiology professor and neurological imaging specialist at the University of Pennsylvania, is a leading figure in the study of the brain biology (neurobiology) of religious experiences. He has used high-tech imaging techniques to observe changes in brain function that occur during meditation and deep prayer. It is thought that his work may ultimately help to show how our minds move beyond the self and open to the divine.

In his book *Why God Won't Go Away* and numerous scientific publications Newberg has described the results of experiments that he and others have carried out. These have demonstrated that prayerful meditation is correlated with a quieting of activity and reduction in blood flow in the posterior superior parietal lobe, an area that lies towards the middle of the brain and is normally responsible for providing us with our sense of orientation. This may indicate how the person meditating is experiencing oneness with the 'sacred' and a loss of boundaries of the self. Studies have also demonstrated that the frontal and temporal areas of the brain become active during meditation.

At the same time various chemical changes have been shown to take place in the blood. There is an increase in melatonin and serotonin levels and a reduction in cortisol (a steroid hormone) and epinephrine levels. This makes sense, as the former two hormones are involved in relaxation, whereas the latter two are increased during physical stress.

During an interview with a magazine, Professor Newberg was asked whether the experiences of people meditating were externally real or not. He explained that scientifically proving the religious reality of his studies might not be possible:

'While I think we have provided the most comprehensive neurological model of meditation and prayer to date, I can't prove or disprove that when somebody connects with God, he or she has actually connected. My publisher originally wanted me to call this a "real" experience – which we have no way of proving. Eventually, we compromised with the term "neurologically real" and we are in fact seeing something that is real from that perspective.'

Ultimately, I realized, all that we experience, including religious experiences and NDEs, is mediated by the brain. Undoubtedly we will one day discover the molecular mediators of religious experiences and NDEs and also the exact areas of the brain that mediate them, but this will only tell us what parts of the brain are involved in the experiences, not whether the experiences are real.

Our brain and our senses limit our ability to determine what is truly real. Therefore we have to move away from thinking about whether NDEs are real or not. We do not have the physical senses to determine whether there is an external reality beyond what we can perceive and we have not yet developed the scientific instruments that will allow us to determine this objectively.

What Causes an NDE?

By now, a large number of the big pieces of the jigsaw had begun to fall into place and a very interesting picture was beginning to emerge. Although undoubtedly more research was needed, I started to think more and more about how it could all be put together. In particular I focused on determining what happens when we die and what causes an NDE to occur. The big questions on my mind were: what are the steps that lead to an NDE and what could be the mechanism that causes the experience to occur?

I started off by looking at all the pieces of evidence that had been found so far. Undoubtedly the central piece of evidence was that at the end of life there was a common subjective experience that was pleasant for the majority and was consistent with previously described NDEs. This experience was not limited to a particular type of person and had been described by people all over the world and also by very small children. Looking back at the evidence, it appeared that the theme of the experience was very much the same for most people and judging from the historical accounts, and particularly the painting by Hieronymus Bosch (see Frontispiece), it had also been present in the Renaissance and at other times. However, although the near death experience shared a number of common and consistent features, it was not the same for everyone; in fact no two experiences were the same.

Looking through the published studies and also the accounts of the people I had met and whose experiences I had examined, it was clear that the experience seemed to occur most commonly in those who were closest to death. Nevertheless it also occurred in others who were less severely ill and sometimes not even severely ill at all. Did this mean that the near death experience was not an experience reflecting the dying process after all?

This aspect of NDEs has been very well demonstrated in an ongoing study by Professor Greyson, in which of almost 1,600 people admitted to a specialist heart service, 10 per cent of those with the most severe and critical illness, i.e. a cardiac arrest, have had an NDE, while the overall occurrence of the phenomenon has persistently decreased in those people who have had less severe forms of cardiac illness. Despite this, the occurrence of NDE has not reached zero in those who are not severely ill, and about 1 per cent of those who have been admitted with non life-threatening heart disease have also had an NDE.

I also realized that there had been many anecdotal reports of NDE-like experiences occurring in people who had not been close to death. In particular the out of body component had been described in many other circumstances, ranging from deep relaxation to severe pain or critical illness.

Although the experience followed a particular pattern which was somewhat consistent in what people saw and experienced, such as a bright light, a tunnel, deceased relatives and even themselves from above, the individuals' own mindset seemed to be a major factor in how they interpreted the experience. For example many people identified the being of light as a religious person such as Jesus, whereas others interpreted it differently and others simply described it as a being of immense love and light. Children also tended to have simpler experiences and their interpretation was based upon the abilities that corresponded to their age.

I remembered back to when I was a child aged four and woke up one night to the sound of a wasp that had got into my bedroom. I was petrified of wasps and being stung by them, so I started to cry and ran round the room trying to avoid the wasp. On one occasion it flew very close to me and I even felt the wind on my face as it went past me. When it got close to me, I tried to beat it away and in my panic I made so much noise that I woke up my father. He came to the room, looking very worried, and said, 'What's the matter?'

Shocked and sobbing, I cried, 'The wasp, the wasp!' and pointed up towards it.

'Where?' he said.

'There, there ... Here it comes!' I cried, as I curled up in his arms.

'But where?' he said. 'It's gone now.'

'There it is – now it's sitting on the ceiling,' I said.

He looked up at the ceiling and said, 'But there's no wasp there.'

'Yes, there is. There it is!' I insisted.

After a few minutes of this, my dad finally smiled at me and said, 'Oh, I see now ... Don't worry, it won't hurt you.'

As I sat there in his arms, feeling secure, I noticed that the wasp wasn't there any more. 'It's gone now,' I said.

'Yes. I told you it wouldn't hurt you. Why don't you go back to sleep again?' my dad suggested.

I made him promise not to leave the room and eventually went to sleep with him sitting up next to me.

I didn't realize it at the time, and in fact it took me many years to realize it, but there had never been a real wasp in the room that night. I must have had a nightmare that had continued even in the waking state. That was why my dad eventually smiled when he realized that I was 'seeing things'. Nevertheless I did see a wasp that was very real to me. I saw it, I heard it and I even felt the wind coming off its wings it as it flew past me.

Seeing, as already mentioned, is a process that takes place through the action of waves of light on the back of the eye, which in turn sends electrical signals to the many areas of the brain that are involved with processing vision. It is the brain that ultimately interprets these signals and gives them meaning. This is why it is possible to see things that aren't there. It is the same with our other senses. So, many years later, I came to understand that on the night that I saw and heard and felt the wasp pass by, the areas of my brain that were involved with sight, sound and touch had all become active in exactly the same way as they would have done if a wasp had really been in the room. This principle applies to all experiences, including NDEs – they are all undoubtedly mediated by the brain.

I thought back to what happens in the body when someone becomes critically ill and approaches death. As already mentioned, numerous physiological changes take place, including a severe reduction in blood pressure as the heart stops beating. There is also a build-up of various toxic chemicals in the body, which cannot be eliminated effectively anymore. This all leads to the release of chemical signals from different cells in the body, including the brain. These chemicals can somehow activate specific areas of the brain (which are likely to be on the surface and around the sides, i.e. the temporal and parietal areas, and possibly the back) that are involved with vision, peacefulness and comfort, and lead to a very vivid and comforting experience. Then something else can also happen and the individual can feel that their consciousness has separated from their brain, so that they can 'see' and 'hear' all that is happening below. They can form long-term memories, reason with themselves and also form lucid, well-structured thought processes. At this point we simply do not know if they develop an illusion of separation from the body, or whether one of those areas of the brain that has been activated somehow leads to a real separation of mind and consciousness from the brain. This is the aspect that can be tested objectively and that I

Summary diagram of what happens when we die

(1) An event such as a severe infection, or accident, or failure of the major organs leads to the blood pressure dropping.

(2) This leads to 'stress' chemical signals being released. These are called 'cytokines'. These chemicals are like the 'language of the cells', and here they release a pattern consistent with severe 'stress'.

(3) This activates many of the 'genes' that code for the production of various hormones such as epinephrine, 'steroids' and endorphins.

(4) These and other potential chemicals activate different parts of the brain. We don't yet know exactly where though.

(5) A specific change in the brain leads to a:

NDE –

But does identifying the chemical changes mean the experience was not real?

had attempted to investigate as part of the pilot study in Southampton.

Now, in order to answer the question of how people could also have NDE-like experiences and out of body experiences when not close to death, I realized that other triggers simply activated the same parts of the brain. This would imply that the chemical mediator and areas of the brain that mediate the experience are not specific to the dying process but can also become activated occasionally under other circumstances, in the same way, for example, that someone can feel a sense of elation when hearing good news, but also when they are given a drug that acts on the same spot on the brain. Neither of these forms of elation negates the validity of the other. They are simply different routes to the same effect.

Given that the brain mediates all our experiences, when someone has an experience they are necessarily bound to relate it according to the symbolism that the brain can construct. Since the brain and senses are limited to perceiving 'reality' in a 3D format, this is probably why people report seeing a tunnel or a gateway. Whatever the nature of the experience may have been, when it is incorporated into the language of the brain it has to be constructed and retold according to the limitations of the processing of the brain. Thus a common language is used.

Although discovering the specific neurological pathways that mediate the near death experience will not prove that the experiences are 'real' or 'unreal', they may be very significant in that they may help to discover new ways to manipulate the brain and mediate the same effects as an NDE. People who suffer with depressive tendencies, for example, may benefit from artificial activation of the same areas of the brain that mediate NDEs.

A major theme of a near death experience is that it has a profoundly religious impact on those who experience it and many of them perform highly altruistic acts afterwards. In addition, as was shown by the study carried out by Dr Van Lommel, it has a very positive life-enhancing effect on people in that they become less materialistic, more altruistic and less afraid of death and develop a faith in God, without necessarily joining a particular religion. Whatever causes the experience, the NDE itself has a very positive long-term effect on those who experience it. This effect is likely to be mediated by long-term brain-based changes in the body too; that would also help to bring about the positive effects. It may be possible to discover these mechanisms scientifically in the future.

At present, however, I realized the only aspect of NDE that was amenable to objective scientific testing was the claims of out of body experiences. This would help us indirectly determine if there was any possibility of a separation of mind and brain at the end of life. This in itself was extremely significant … So, while I pursued the different avenues of research, I also prepared for our large-scale study of the near death experience during cardiac arrest.

8

The Horizon

Except for a few clouds on the horizon, there was blue sky all the way ahead. As I stared at it, for a moment I occupied myself with my own thoughts. This was almost how I saw our project. Although there were some clouds ahead, I felt confident that the sky would clear. *We'll see*, I thought to myself. *Now I wonder where we are?*

I glanced down at the map and then looked below to see if I could find the town that we were passing over. *That must be it … I wonder if we are in Switzerland now?* I certainly hoped so! I had spent almost six hours in a little propeller plane that belonged to Dr Peter Fenwick. We were on our way to meet members of a German/Swiss charity. They had shown interest in our work and had invited us to their headquarters in Kreuzlingen, a small town outside Zurich, to see whether they could help us raise funds for the second stage of our research project.

This trip was one of many attempts that I made to raise funds to build on our pilot study and conduct the first ever large-scale study of NDE in cardiac arrest in the world. We hoped that this study would be the definitive study needed to investigate the outcome of the human mind and consciousness at the end of life.

By this time I had completed my training in internal medicine, passed my final postgraduate (MRCP) examination and had started working towards a PhD on some of the molecular mechanisms involved in lung disease. I had decided to try and combine a career in academic as well as clinical, respiratory and intensive care medicine. I knew this meant that during the next three years I would have to give up most of my spare time. Since I had to work on my PhD project during the day as well as see patients in clinic and do some on-calls in hospital, I would essentially be left with just a few hours free in the evenings and some weekends. Nevertheless, I thought it was worth it. Since I had now been drawn into this field, I really wanted to solve the mystery once and for all. I couldn't just abandon it.

I was working under Stephen Holgate, one of the most respected professors in the field of asthma research. He had a worldwide reputation for excellence and had been approached for many high profile jobs, such as Chief Medical Officer in the UK and also head of pulmonary medicine at Harvard Medical School in the USA. I also worked under Professor Donna Davies, a very talented and highly experienced researcher, and Professor Anthony Frew, an expert on asthma and allergic disorders.

Stephen Holgate was an extremely kind and approachable man. He had a real way with people and everybody both respected and admired him. He was also altruistic. After I started working in his department, he enthusiastically agreed to support my proposed NDE study as well.

This time we couldn't do the study on just a shoestring budget and so we needed to apply for a research fund. We would have to raise the necessary funds in the first year and then concentrate on doing the study in the next two years. Based upon our pilot study in Southampton, we calculated that we would need to study approximately 1,500 cardiac arrest survivors and in order to complete the study in two years would need to recruit 25 hospitals to help with it. I hoped that once we had raised the funds, then we could recruit research nurses to work under my supervision. This way I would be able to spend more time on my PhD, especially in the second and third years when it was going to get tougher, and still get the NDE project done. I knew this was an ambitious plan, but I thought it was worth trying.

In early 2000, I worked with Dr Peter Fenwick, Dr Derek Waller and Professor Stephen Holgate to submit our first grant application for funding. We decided to apply to a charity that was one of the biggest and best-known medical funding bodies in the UK. At that time they had a grant available that was designed to support high-risk yet novel and innovative studies and I felt confident that they would fund our study. My confidence stemmed from the fact that it *was* both novel and innovative and had never been attempted anywhere in the world. In addition we were investigating a really new area of medicine that was truly exciting.

To my delight, our application was received warmly by the charity. I was told over the telephone that during their assessment the committee had looked at it very favourably and that pending a few questions and minor modifications, it would be approved. It was commonplace and certainly nothing unusual for a committee to raise a few questions before a final approval. The application had also been sent out to other scientists for review and they too responded positively. We seemed to be on track.

Bizarrely, and rather worryingly, however, it took almost six months for the committee's questions to be sent to us. This was a very straightforward and standard procedure, so why was it taking so long? During these months I contacted the charity on numerous occasions, only to be told that the matter was being dealt with and that the application had gone to a different office for review.

Once we had finally received the questions, we replied to them and made the requested amendments to the proposal, but after an acknowledgement letter, yet again months went by with no specific reply. There really was something wrong! During this time I often spoke with the office staff who dealt with these applications, but they kept on saying that ours had gone to another desk and a very senior member of the charity was now reviewing it.

Eventually, after more than 18 months of waiting, our application was rejected. In the final letter, no real reason was given, but just before we received it I had managed to speak to the scientific director in charge of the programme and he had actually told me that the charity was concerned that NDE research might have a negative impact in the press on their organization and that for this reason they wouldn't be able to support it. He also suggested that I should not pursue this type of research myself, as it would not be good for my career. I was really gutted. There had been no problems with the scientific reviews, so why had they taken this negative view? I was really very disappointed indeed.

Also, it had been a long wait to get the reply. If they had just rejected it at the beginning then I wouldn't have minded so much, but now we had lost 18 months waiting for them to make a decision. I was also upset because I felt the project wasn't being rejected on scientific grounds but simply due to prejudice. In addition, unfortunately for us, during this 18 months we had not been allowed to apply anywhere else. Now I had to abandon all plans to start the research and go back to the drawing board again.

I looked for alternative sources of funding, but it wasn't easy. Normally when a scientist wants to fund a study, they have to apply to a medical charity that has a remit to fund research in that area. There were charities for cancer care, heart disease, lung disease, diabetes, etc. – everything really, except NDE. Not only this, but very few charities were interested in the subject of death and dying and those that were either had no research budget or a very limited one.

Although our first application had been to a major charity with a specific grant designed to fund high-risk or what was commonly termed 'blue sky' research, this was an exception, as most charities only funded well-established 'low-risk' projects. They had adopted this strategy in recent times in order to maximize the use of donations. Although this was good in many ways, there was also a downside, and I was experiencing it. Much of scientific progress had come through blue sky research projects and this new strategy would stifle researchers with untested ideas. However, I couldn't change the system, I just had to work with it.

Then I had an idea. There were obviously many people interested in near death experiences, but there were no charities that funded research into the subject. So why not try to establish a charity ourselves? I had seen how many research departments, including Stephen Holgate's, had set up their own local charities, so why couldn't we do the same? This way anybody who was interested would be able to make donations and we could also perhaps liaise with other charities to fund NDE research. Maybe we could not only fund our own study but also become a source of funding for other people who wanted to research NDEs.

When I spoke to Peter about it, he told me that in the 1980s he and a few others had set up a charity together which had now become completely dormant. 'Why don't you take it over and reactivate it?' he said. So I did.

The first person I contacted for help with this was Heather Sloan. Heather was a real angel who had helped me so much with my NDE work. We had met when she had written to me with her own NDE and I had invited her for an interview. When I was looking for someone to help with my NDE work, I had asked her and she had kindly agreed. Better still, she had now started a new secretarial job at the hospital, making it easy for us to meet regularly. I told Heather about the charity and she agreed to help. She quickly and enthusiastically set up an office at home and we renamed the charity Horizon Research Foundation. We were up and running!

There was a real need for a charity like Horizon, as there were many people who had had NDEs but had nowhere to turn for help in the UK. It became a very exciting time for us indeed. We created a new logo and then started working on establishing a newsletter and membership scheme. One of my friends, Fred, kindly donated his time and created and maintained a website for us. During the following years Sarah, a friend of Heather's, and Kirsti, a lady who had contacted us directly, also helped modify and maintain it. We eventually had a great team of volunteers all working together.

Heather carried the biggest workload. She managed all our administration and the office as well as speaking to all the people who contacted us with NDEs. She had great rapport and kindness and really comforted those who had had traumatic experiences. She worked entirely selflessly and I grew to admire Heather more and more as time went by. She had wonderful qualities and was truly altruistic. Also on days when there was a story about our work in the media, she would get others in to man the telephones. Soon after we had set up Horizon, I appeared on the morning programme GMTV and we were inundated with calls. Luckily, Heather had got a team ready to take them all, including 'Grandma', her elderly mother.

The rest of our team of volunteers included Cassie Wilcox, a very creative writer who helped with the production of our newsletters, Giti Amirani, a young dynamic Oxford graduate with excellent experience of working with charities, and Brenda North, who worked with the pharmaceutical industry. They all helped tremendously and worked tirelessly with affection and enthusiasm. I felt honoured. We really had a great team.

We deliberately decided to keep the membership costs of Horizon as low as possible, so we charged £10 per year, which gave members four newsletters annually and also discount on any events. The newsletters provided light-hearted news about NDEs and also any other interesting news, as well as an update on our progress with the study.

We also organized an annual conference where we could update people on the latest progress in NDE research. The first was held in Southampton in the autumn of 2001 and the second a year later in London. We had a great turnout and on both occasions the lecture theatres were full. Amazingly, Heather and I organized the first one together. For the second conference we had more help, as by then we had been joined by Giti, Cassie and Brenda. We all worked extremely hard to organize these conferences and Giti in particular did a great job with PR. She got our conference covered in *The Times* as well as on *Breakfast*, the morning news programme on BBC1. Many other reports followed, including one in *The Australian* newspaper.

During these years, we had many wonderful times. I started travelling around the country giving talks to other doctors. These were mainly evening dinner sessions that had been sponsored by a pharmaceutical company and had two benefits: first, they made doctors more aware of NDEs; and second, they provided a funding stream for Horizon through the speaker's fees, which I gave to the charity.

During this time I was also invited to give a lecture by Dr Lili Feng, a researcher at the prestigious Baylor College of Medicine in Houston, Texas, who was studying the changes that take place in the body's genes in response to disease. She was also keen to study these changes in response to changes in the mind. This way, she hoped to map out the intermediary gene and molecular changes in the body that take place during different states of mind. She had completed a small study looking at gene changes in response to meditation and now she was interested in whether we could also extend this principle to studying the changes that take place when people have a near death experience.

'After people have an NDE, they are transformed very positively by the experience and generally become happier, more altruistic people,' she argued. 'I wonder if we can discover the changes that are taking place at the level of the genes in their body after an NDE. If we can discover the genes that are mediating these changes, then perhaps we can use this technology to help other people too.'

Her aim was to identify the brain-based changes that accompany an NDE and then try and artificially stimulate these in people with depression. That was a wonderful idea, but undoubtedly very difficult to carry out in real life.

During that trip, I was also invited to give lectures at the Harvard Science Center in Boston and UCLA (the University of California at Los Angeles) and Caltech (the California Institute of Technology), both in Los Angeles. The title of my lecture was 'Near death experiences in cardiac arrest: visions of a dying brain or visions of a new science of consciousness?' At Caltech there was a large scientific group interested in the problem of consciousness and although I had been invited by the biological sciences department, a large number of students and faculty from the consciousness group also came to the lecture. For me this was the most stimulating session I had ever had, as these people were very interested in the problem of consciousness and were in fact at the forefront of studying the neural correlates of consciousness.

The organizers at Caltech had also sent out a press release about the event and during my short stay in Los Angeles I was interviewed by Sarah Tippit, a reporter for Reuters news agency. The interview was released globally and so overnight reports of our work appeared in places as far away as Hungary, Turkey, China and India. One of my closest friends told me his father had even seen us on the front cover of a newspaper in Nigeria!

Near death experiences were certainly very popular all over the world. There was no doubt about that. When I had first started my research I hadn't expected quite so much interest, but I could see now that there was truly global interest in the subject.

'Ere, Norm! You had one of them near-death experiences once, didn't you?

I also found this cartoon that appeared in the *Daily Mail* very amusing! I really enjoyed the light-hearted approach that some cartoonists had taken to the subject of near death experiences. (*Source:* Reproduced by kind permission of Solo Syndication.)

I had experienced my first taste of this a year earlier when I had been waiting to get the results of our Southampton study published in the medical journal *Resuscitation*. Then I had been contacted by Jonathan Petre, a journalist working for the *Sunday Telegraph* in London, who had asked about our study. When he had found out that no one had yet reported our results, he had excitedly asked me to let him have an exclusive interview. The following week, when his article was published, there had been a surge of telephone calls from members of the press both to work and to the university press office. I had not been expecting this and was actually away from work at the time. So I spent that entire week giving interviews, either via satellite link to Australia and Canada, where we had been on the front page of the newspapers, or in person. I also had a team from RAI, the Italian television network, visit me, and since the reporter was a keen football fan and covered all Italian news in the UK, I learned a lot about the many Italian football stars who lived and worked in London.

On the day that Reuters released news of our study, their article was the no.1 article on Yahoo in terms of hits and number of times it was copied and e-mailed to others. There were also more than 500 posts to the Yahoo! website, and the BBC, together with the Discovery Channel, contacted me to ask me to help with the production of a new documentary called *The Day I Died*.

Despite the global, public and media interest, however, we had still not managed to get the second stage of our research funded. Also, although the work of Horizon was a great success, it was extremely time-consuming for me. Even though we had a great team, I still had to input a lot of the materials. Our second conference had taken four months to organize and it was getting very hard for me to cope with all the work that I had to do. I had a very limited amount of spare time and I still had to try and raise funds for the NDE study. Unfortunately I couldn't delegate this to anyone else, as it needed scientific writing. My other problem was that the pressure with my thesis was also building up. I had only 18 months left and if I wanted to succeed I had to spend many of my evenings and weekends working in the lab. It was getting to a point where I would have to decide between my PhD and Horizon.

By early 2003, we had managed to raise some funds through Horizon, but only very modest amounts indeed. Also, Heather's personal circumstances had changed. Her husband had become quite ill and so had her elderly mother. She would get home from work and then have to attend to her husband and to her mother, who lived nearby, as well as do her work for Horizon, and it was wearing her out. When we had started we had hoped that we could raise enough money to employ an administrator and a fundraiser, but the reality was that we couldn't. And now, reluctantly, Heather and I had to face the fact that neither of us could dedicate so much time to Horizon. We decided to complete one year's newsletters, so that those who had paid would get their money's worth, and then not cash anybody else's money. We would have to slowly cease activity with Horizon until our circumstances changed.

During those three years I had worked very hard at raising funds for the NDE research and had applied to many organizations, but with little success. The problem was really that there were no organizations with research funds available that were interested in funding research into the dying process. More often than not, the feedback was that although interesting, this wasn't an area that they were looking to fund. I could understand their position – they had to fund what lay in their own remit.

Despite the many unsuccessful attempts to raise the funds needed for the larger study, however, we had made some real progress in understanding more about what happens when we die. We had been the first group to relate near death experiences during cardiac arrest to the study of consciousness and to highlight the important changes that take place in the brain during cardiac arrest. I had reviewed this in a scientific article written together with Peter Fenwick for the medical journal *Resuscitation* in 2002. There was also definite medical interest in the subject. According to the journal, our article was one of the most popular that year. I had managed to form a scientific group to study consciousness at the University of Southampton and had been invited to give a number of lectures in the UK, including for the Resuscitation Council, the Intensive Care Society and the British Psychological Society. I had also become a reviewer on the subject for *The New England Journal of Medicine*, possibly the most prestigious medical journal in the world.

Despite the many obstacles, perhaps one of the sweetest moments for me during that three-year period was when Paul, the 16-year-old son of one of my friends, told me that he and his classmates had been taught about our work at school. They had also been shown a video of the BBC documentary *The Day I Died*. Soon afterwards I was contacted by a publishing company who informed that they were writing about our work in the latest edition of an educational textbook for schoolchildren. The fact that our work had trickled down to the schools and was being taught to our youngsters really gave me a great sense of happiness.

RESEARCH ON THE HORIZON

After my lecture at the Resuscitation Council annual conference in London, some of the members of the Resuscitation Council Committee were very excited by it, and actually came up to me and suggested that I apply to the council for funding of my study. They did warn me that they had a very limited budget, but said that at least it would be a start. So I applied and finally, after almost three years of trying to raise funds, I managed to get a small grant from the Resuscitation Council to further the study of NDE and the human mind during cardiac arrest.

We had initially sought to raise over £140,000 to recruit three research nurses to help us enrol over 1,500 cardiac arrest survivors in two years. Our aim had been to characterize their experiences, construct a new NDE scale and study the possible factors causing NDE in more detail. Now we had less funding and so we had to scale back and try and build up slowly.

Another problem was that my personal circumstances had changed. Initially, I had been hoping to start the study right at the beginning of my PhD project. Then I had more time; now I was under a lot of pressure to complete my experiments and write up my PhD thesis. I also had a new clinical job starting at Hammersmith Hospital in London, so before I could start the study I really had to complete my PhD.

I often wondered what would have happened if our larger study had been funded three years earlier. The potential was immense, but I couldn't dwell on that too much. I had tried my best, but it hadn't quite worked out as I had hoped.

Now, however, as I write this book, I have completed my PhD thesis and together with Dr Peter Fenwick and Ken Spearpoint, a very bright and knowledgeable senior resuscitation officer, we are about start a new and truly novel study exploring what happens when we die. This is being funded by the Resuscitation Council and so will start on a small scale. We have improved our technology and so it has become a little more expensive, but, should we manage to raise the necessary funds, which are in the region of £200,000, we will be able to complete the work as planned in 1,500 cardiac arrest survivors.

This new study, which will be the largest and most comprehensive NDE study to date, is being built on the work carried out during the pilot study in Southampton. Its aim is to use the latest available EEG and brain monitoring technology to study exactly what happens to the brain during the dying process. We will then be able to measure brain activity precisely and relate this to the reports of consciousness during cardiac arrest to determine whether consciousness really can exist during a brain 'flatline'.

We will also be able to record and test the reports of being able to see from above during a cardiac arrest through a technological refinement using random images that will only be visible from a vantage point above. These will then be used to correlate reports of consciousness during cardiac arrest with recorded brain activity.

We also aim to study the psychological and biochemical factors that may impact on the occurrence of an experience and the brain-based molecular changes that may impact on the nature of the experience and may mediate the long-term positive effects of the experience.

Like any study, this will of course depend on many factors, including adequate funding and collaboration; however, the major point is that the technology exists to indirectly test the nature of human consciousness and what happens to it at the end of life.

Should it all go as planned, the results of this study should be available in the not too distant future. Moreover, it will be possible for other researchers to carry out similar work independently and confirm any findings in the coming years. In the meantime, Peter Fenwick and I are actively looking for collaborators in academic centres worldwide to work on various aspects relating to research in the area of what happens at the end of life and are actively developing a website through the Horizon Research Foundation.

9

Implications for the Future

As I sit here writing this book, I am about to embark on a new adventure in my life. A new page is about to be turned and I am about to leave the country in which I grew up and which I love to go to another. I will be leaving behind close family and friends and many special memories. I am going to take up a new post in pulmonary and critical care medicine at Cornell University's Presbyterian Hospital in New York. There I will continue to work in clinical medicine as well as do research into the molecular mechanisms of cell and gene function. The hospital is at the forefront of developments in gene therapy and I am sure that I will explore the secrets that lie in human genes in great depth, searching not only for new medical treatments but also for the answers to the mysteries of human consciousness. I will also continue with my research into what happens at the end of life.

Isn't it strange that my story commenced with a visit to another famous New York hospital 10 years earlier? Now I can look back and say that the questions that Desmond raised in my mind all those years ago have led to real medical progress. So, as I look back, I think to myself, *Well, what have we learned so far?*

We have confirmed that at the very least the dying process is a pleasant experience for the majority. Although there had been many reports of NDEs in the past, the move by researchers, including our team at Southampton, Dr Van Lommel, Dr Schwaninger and Professor Greyson, to study these experiences 'prospectively' at the objective point of death proved to be a major advance over previous 'retrospective' approaches. Interestingly, these studies have shown that a proportion of people report having lucid, well-structured thought processes with reasoning and memory formation at a time when there should be none. This has raised many intriguing questions regarding the relationship between the mind and the brain.

In an editorial in the prestigious medical journal *The Lancet*, Professor French, a psychologist at the University of London, concluded that: 'The nature of mind–brain relationships and the possibility of life-after-death are some of the most profound issues relating to mankind's place in the universe. The report ... of near-death experiences in survivors of a cardiac arrest provides intriguing data that are relevant to these issues.'

Could we now be on the verge of discovering the nature of human consciousness? Scientific mysteries do indeed take many centuries to solve, but could this be the first clue to the puzzle? I believe it is. For centuries the nature of consciousness has been considered a purely philosophical issue, yet now it has become one of the biggest challenges facing neuroscience. Once an 'unconventional' area of scientific study, it has now been debated in some of the most highly respected scientific circles.

What is without doubt is that this question is important to us all. Consciousness encompasses every moment of our lives and all our interactions with others. It allows us to know joy or sorrow, happiness or sadness, to feel a sense of shame or pride, to experience a moment of remorse. It gives us higher faculties such as forgiveness, love, compassion and a moral conscience. It is what allows us to sacrifice our comfort and happiness, or even life, for the love of another. Simply think of our relationships with our loved ones. We interact with each other through our minds, thoughts and feelings. This is also true on a larger scale when we look at the way that we conduct ourselves in society. The problem facing science today is where does our consciousness – our free will, conscience, feelings, thoughts and emotions – actually come from and how is it produced?

STEPS TOWARDS SOLVING THE MYSTERY OF CONSCIOUSNESS

Without doubt the brain plays a pivotal and essential role in consciousness. We know this because if there is damage to a certain part of the brain following for example a stroke or a head injury, very specific mental functions may be lost, such as memory, or the ability to recognize others, or the ability to form sentences. We know this doesn't happen with any other organ in the body and so we can definitely conclude that it is the brain that is involved.

This has been confirmed in recent years with the advent of brain-scanning techniques such as functional MRI and PET, which have helped to map out the areas of the brain that are involved in these functions. We have found a direct correlation between the mind, consciousness and the brain, but it is only a correlation and not proof of how the mind comes to exist. As with any correlation, we have to ask the question: does A lead to B, or does B lead to A? We know that there is brain cell activity in relation to the mind, but which way is the relationship? Is it the brain cells that activate the mind, or is it the mind that activates the brain cells, or could it even be both? Which comes first, the chicken or the egg, the brain or the mind? If we want to be purely scientific, we must keep an open mind and not let our own personal biases cloud our judgement. We should let the evidence guide us.

The majority of scientists currently support the view that brain processes somehow lead to the formation of consciousness. As outlined earlier, many different intermediary brain centres and pathways have been proposed to account for this. There are, however, other scientists, including the Nobel Prize winning neuroscientist Professor Eccles, who have supported the theory that the mind is a separate entity that cannot be reduced down to brain cell processes. Some have argued that we will never be able to account for the formation of consciousness through the electrical and chemical processes of the brain. So which of the scientific views is correct?

Until fairly recently I used to believe that brain processes led to the formation of consciousness and the mind, although like all the other scientists, I did not know how. However, studying near death experiences in cardiac arrest survivors has made me question my views, as has the lack of plausible biological mechanisms to account for the causation of consciousness from brain processes. I have now decided to keep a completely open mind and let the evidence sway my opinion. After all, this wouldn't be the first time in science that a prevailing view has been proved wrong. When we look back, we can see that many widely accepted theories have been modified or even completely changed in the light of new evidence. Personally, I have had to accept that the formation of consciousness is far from clear and it could be that the latter view is correct.

So how do the reports of NDE in cardiac arrest help the research into consciousness? Numerous studies have shown that thought processes are mediated by multiple areas of the brain and not just a single area. For this, brain cells need to communicate, using electrical pulses. During cardiac arrest there is a severe insult to the brain that causes either no blood flow to the brain or at best severely reduced blood flow. Either way, there is such a deficiency in blood flow that electrical activity in the brain ceases within a few seconds and there remains a flatline throughout the period of the cardiac arrest and even afterwards for some people. Nevertheless, some formal thought processes and consciousness appear to be present in a proportion of those who are in cardiac arrest.

In normal medical practice, it is well recognized that any alteration in the function of the brain leads to a clouded sense of consciousness, which is highlighted by a confusional state, and if the impairment is more significant, consciousness is lost. All we have to do is spend an evening in an emergency department and we will see that people who have any significant alteration in the level of nutrients and/or chemicals around the brain become confused. This can take place with any illness, whether pneumonia, a heart attack, diabetes or an infection around the brain. This is the basis of all mental tests on patients who have become acutely unwell. If such conditions are left untreated, they can lead to a coma. However, in all these conditions, the insult is still not so great as to cause the brainwaves to go flat. At worst they start to show changes in shape. How is it then that we have a clinical scenario in which there is severe brain dysfunction, the worst possible type, with an absence of electrical activity in the brain, but somehow thought processes, with reasoning, memory formation and consciousness continue and are even heightened?

It might be suggested that the thoughts are arising from a small area of the brain that is somehow able to receive blood flow, however numerous studies have demonstrated that thought processes are generated by global brain function, also it is almost impossible for one area to receive blood when there is hardly any blood flow to the brain. Scientifically speaking, there should be no consciousness present at all. How then can we account for the findings of NDE research? As Dr Van Lommel stated, 'How could a clear conscious-ness outside one's body be experienced at the moment that the brain no longer functions during a period of clinical death with flat EEG?'

The most obvious explanation seems to be that perhaps the experience isn't occurring during the period of cardiac arrest after all. Dr Susan Blackmore and Professor Christopher French, two British psychologists, have suggested that it may be occurring just before the crisis, or even just after, when the individual is still in an unconscious state but blood flow is relatively normal and brainwaves are present. Obviously, as the heart stops, there will be a period of a few seconds before blood flow is stopped to the brain, and after the heart recovers, there will be a period in which there is relatively normal blood flow to the brain before the person actually awakens. As memories and thoughts can take place in an instant, Blackmore and French have proposed that NDEs may also be occurring just before or after the event, but the individuals concerned *think* they happened during the main part of the cardiac arrest itself.

This is possible, however there have been many individuals who have recalled details from the middle of the cardiac arrest, when brain blood flow has been shown to be severely impaired. Think of the examples that were given to me by Drs Mansfield, La Rovere and Professor Chamberlain. In cases such as these, we can't say that the experience was happening at the beginning or end of the cardiac arrest, as the patients recalled details of what was happening during the cardiac arrest.

This is therefore an area that needs to be investigated in more detail. We need to be able to time the experiences accurately. Both Dr Blackmore and Professor French agree that if clear consciousness were possible with a completely flat EEG this would indeed change our view of the mind brain relationship, but so far this has not been conclusively demonstrated.

From a scientific point of view, studying the human mind at the physiological point of death, when global blood flow, and hence brain function, have become severely impaired, is currently the best and possibly the only method to study the relationship between the mind and the brain. Should consciousness truly be present during this time, then this raises a very interesting point. If mind and consciousness are products of brain activity, then they would be expected to also cease functioning at this time, or at best very shortly afterwards. It is a little like going into a room in which there is a light and not knowing where the light is coming from. If we turn the switch off at the wall and the light goes off, then we can conclude that the light was coming from the bulb we had turned off. If on the other hand we switch it off and the light is still present, then we have to conclude that it must have been coming from another source.

So far we do not have definitive proof for either theory. However, as many thousands of people, including small children, have reported a fully functioning mind and consciousness and have been able to watch specific details that were happening during their cardiac arrest, the possibility is raised that mind and consciousness can exist separately from the brain and also during and at least for some time after death. There are also many anecdotal reports from medical professionals who have resuscitated patients who have upon recovery told them the details of what happened during their cardiac arrest.

The problem is that so far there have been no studies with adequate numbers of patients to investigate this phenomenon fully. When we look for a significant effect with a new drug, we sometimes have to study thousands of subjects, and the same is true with consciousness at the end of life. It is up to us as scientists to investigate these claims adequately and with appropriate studies, which are now possible. It is also for funding bodies to support such novel research, which could have profound implications for us all. If we take up this challenge then we can potentially answer the last completely unsolved mystery in biological sciences.

What then of the various brain-based theories to account for NDEs and consciousness? There is no doubt that the body affects the mind and consciousness and also that the mind and consciousness affect the brain and body. The most important point, as I have come to realize, is that identifying the brain-based chemical changes that accompany any subjective feeling or activity of consciousness will not be likely to tell us if an experience is real or not. It will simply give us the intermediaries that are needed to manifest a subjective event or feeling. This of course also applies to the study of the neural correlates of near death experiences. Finding the intermediary pathways and chemicals will not be able to tell us if an experience is real or not.

In light of the evidence from cardiac arrest survivors and the large amount of anecdotal evidence that has accumulated, we now need to test the nature of consciousness during cardiac arrest, when brain function is at best severely impaired or at worst ceased. This is now medically possible and will at least tell us which of the broad views regarding the relationship between the mind, consciousness and brain is correct.

As related earlier, we planned to set up such a large trial, but without adequate funding it could not be done. We wanted to install specially developed devices which would generate many random images at any one time, so that no one would know exactly which images had been shown at any given moment. While I was working at Hammersmith Hospital last year, one of my neurology colleagues, Dr Barry Seemungle, suggested that if we used more than one image with each device, this would make a positive response even more significant, statistically. 'If there were, say, five images and someone identified all five of them it would be almost impossible statistically for it to happen by chance alone ... The odds would be millions to one,' he said. The devices would also have been connected to accurately record the events.

In this way, if a large group of cardiac arrest survivors had been studied and had reported out of body experiences, together with the ability to see events from above, we would have expected them to have also identified the images accurately. If they could have done this, then we would have had to re-examine our views about the relationship between the mind and brain. If, on the other hand, a large group of people had all claimed to be out of body but had not been able to identify the images then we would have had to conclude that they had imagined being at the ceiling. This would have then supported the theory that mind and consciousness are products of the brain and that out of body experiences are simply illusions.

Now we aim to start this study on a small scale and to raise the funds needed to expand it into a very large study in the near future.

COULD MIND AND CONSCIOUSNESS BE SEPARATE FROM THE BRAIN?

Now the question that I have often asked myself is, what would we do if the experiment were carried out and independently replicated by other scientists and it were discovered that the mind and consciousness were separate from the brain? This would obviously have huge implications for us all. How could we account for this and what effect would it have on our lives?

As science progresses, novel ways of 'seeing' and measuring the world around us are developed. At the turn of the twentieth century the use of X-rays began to revolutionize the practice of medicine. For the first time doctors could see inside the body. Then, as science progressed, other methods were devised, such as ultrasound technology, where sound waves are passed through the body. This is still commonly used to perform scans, particularly of the abdomen, and any mother will recall the ultrasound scan of her unborn baby. In more recent times magnetic resonance imaging has enabled us to see inside the body to an accuracy of only a few millimetres. Unfortunately, at present there are no devices available that will allow us to see and measure thoughts and consciousness. However, in view of the enormous progress that has taken place in medicine, and particularly medical physics, I am sure that in time such a device will be developed. Then perhaps we can quite easily discover the nature of consciousness and its relation to the brain, but for now we have to use indirect means to study it. Nevertheless, we do know that mind and consciousness exist and therefore should be amenable to scientific measurement and study. It is just a matter of when and not if.

When we examine the world around us, we see that all beings are made up of billions of molecules combined together. I am an amazing collection of billions of different molecules, which are themselves made up of a combination of different atoms. When I think further down, I know that at the subatomic level and in the quantum world, everything exists in the form of waves. Therefore at the very lowest level, all that we are is in the form of waves, not just our physical body, but also our consciousness and thoughts.

Therefore, I have often wondered whether consciousness is itself a very subtle type of matter that is still not amenable to measurement by our scientific tools. Professor Elahi, a supporter of the view that mind and consciousness are separate from the brain, has suggested that consciousness is made of a very subtle type of matter, similar to electromagnetic waves. This may be a very good analogy, as an electromagnetic wave is indeed a subtle type of matter that is not perceived by our physical senses, but of course exists and can be manifested and 'seen' using the correct apparatus, including television and radio. Scientists only discovered electromagnetic waves in the nineteenth century and the first use of radio waves was over 20 years later. Nevertheless electromagnetic waves have always existed, it was just that science had not yet discovered the means to measure them and use the technology. This is the same for all discoveries. The science behind all of them has existed since the beginning of time, it is just that we are only capable of piecing it together very slowly.

To go back to electromagnetic waves for a moment, interestingly from a medical point of view, they can interact with cells in the body. Many studies have shown that subtle types of matter such as ultraviolet light can directly activate cells and cause them to alter their responses just as other chemical messaging systems do. This may account for how the subtle 'undiscovered' mind/consciousness may interact with brain cells and lead to the measurable alterations that are seen in those cells and their connections as consciousness develops. It has been noted that as we learn, the connections between the brain cells in specific areas related to that process become more complex.

In effect the position that we are currently in regarding the mind and brain is similar to that of a small child who is watching a presenter on a television set. If she doesn't understand how a television works, she may believe that the presenter is actually sitting in the set. She can test this theory by pulling a few wires out of the television and, sure enough, there will be a loss of sound or picture, thus confirming that all that is being seen and heard is coming from the television. Yet although it is possible that the presenter, or 'mind and consciousness', is coming from the set, it is also possible that the set is simply acting as a receiver and manifesting what are subtle forms of electromagnetic waves. Yes, we need the set to see those waves, but it is just a decoder. The actual presenter is possibly sitting thousands of miles away.

By studying consciousness at the end of life, we can see whether anything remains independent of the brain, in which case the brain is only acting like the television set, or whether everything is extinguished by shutting down the brain, in which case we must conclude that the brain is producing the mind and consciousness.

Throughout the entire history of scientific progress there have been numerous examples of very significant shifts in the scientific 'belief system' in light of the emergence of new evidence. These paradigm shifts have often taken place in a very slow manner and very often if not always they are rejected until the evidence has become strong enough to convince most people that it is correct. These 'new beliefs' are usually essential scientific concepts that have been completely unknown and therefore not considered until someone has eventually discovered them. It is very likely that a paradigm shift is needed if our quest to discover the nature of human consciousness is to bear fruit.

THE IMPLICATIONS FOR ETHICS, THEOLOGY AND PHILOSOPHY

As we commence the twenty-first century, one of the most interesting observable changes in science has been the widening of its boundaries to encompass a number of traditionally philosophical questions. These questions have largely been thrust upon science as a direct result of its own progress. Recent discoveries and the consequent improvements in medical care have revealed a maze of ethical issues which were formerly reserved for philosophical debate. Many now feel that the progress of science, although undoubtedly bringing benefits, has itself begun to threaten the sanctity of human life.

If we were to assume that aspects of consciousness were simply products of brain cell activity and the environment, what would this do to our social fabric? What would this do to the notion of free will and accountability? What would this do to our judicial services? At the very extreme it would mean that no one would be held accountable for their actions, as it would be their brain cells and environment that would have 'made them do it'. This of course is not the reality of life in society and we will become fully aware of it if we try to throw a brick through the window of the most reductionist of neuroscientists! In reality, we do have free will and are accountable for our actions.

My view is that ultimately everything, including issues that may be considered theological or philosophical, is amenable to the objective assessment of science. I acknowledge that should it be discovered that mind or consciousness can exist at the end of life and independently of the brain, this would support the theological and philosophical concept of an 'afterlife' and would suggest that the age-old concept of the 'soul' is the same as what scientists now call 'consciousness'. In my opinion the term we use is not relevant, but it is important to study the process scientifically. If consciousness were discovered to be a separate scientific entity, similar to electro-magnetic waves, then it would be amenable to scientific study. As Professor Elahi has suggested, the study of consciousness or the 'soul' would then be treated like any other science with its own axioms, laws and theorems. This would lead to the objective study by science of what has traditionally been considered religious and philosophical subjects, thus potentially ending many disagreements and leading to a far more tolerant society. In the same way that science has revolutionized our understanding of the external world around us, it could also revolutionize our understanding of the subjective world inside us.

Before the institutionalization of science, which started with pioneering scientists such as Galileo and Newton, anybody could claim to be correct on any issue. All the progress that we have made in discovering both the world around us and the intricate inner world that exists inside us owes its existence to the objective method of study that was started around 500 years ago. I believe that we now need to apply the same objectivity as our forefathers, put aside personal and philosophical bias and start by conducting the experiments that would potentially allow us to discover the nature of human consciousness.

THE IMPLICATIONS FOR MEDICAL CARE

The study of NDE in cardiac arrest may also have significant benefits for the treatment of many illnesses, including depression. Although

Dr Lili Feng's idea of discovering the neural mediators of the transformational effect of NDEs will not be easy to carry out, it may be possible. People who have had an NDE are certainly left with a very positive effect that makes them less materialistic, less afraid of death and more altruistic, and these effects are undoubtedly mediated by changes in the expression of genes and specific mediator proteins. The discovery of these molecules could allow us to discover novel ways to treat psychological and psychiatric illnesses and in effect would allow us to instil the positive effects of NDEs in those who have not had them. After discovering the brain signals that are involved with the positive transformational effects of NDEs, we could design drugs that would stimulate the same areas and get the same effect in people who have lost hope and become apathetic. There has been enormous progress recently in the study of the behavioural and dynamic changes that take place in the gene profile in response to different behavioural states. Significant and ever-evolving biochemical technologies now make it possible to study the activities of hundreds of genes at the same time. Since genes are constantly being activated in response to all sorts of stimuli, modern gene chips have allowed large-scale studies of genes and their changes at any given time.

Another benefit will be that once we discover the actual nature of the mind we may well discover alternative means of treating its illnesses. Current medical treatment is focused largely on chemical treatment, however this only works to a limited extent. If we discover that there is a separate component that is of a different nature from chemicals, then we may also be able to discover ways to manipulate it directly.

I would like to end this book with a poignant real-life story about John, an active slim middle-aged man whom I met a few years ago. He was a jovial man who had seen much of the world but had recently been diagnosed with an incurable illness. When we first met, there was a sense of anticipation in his eyes. He had come to hospital with lots of hope for the future. His mood was vibrant, cheery and upbeat. He was chatty with the staff and used to joke and laugh with them. We expected his treatment to bring about some improvement, but unfortunately as time went by we all began to realize that his was a very resistant form of disease and that in his case there was going to be no response.

As time passed on, understandably John began to look more and more dejected and downbeat. In his eyes I could see fear of the future. It was as if he was watching his last glimmers of hope fading away along with his life. Even though his family was there every day to comfort and support him, inwardly he was alone.

One evening I met John looking particularly down and low. I asked what had happened and he told me that although he had suspected it for a while, that day he had finally been given the news that there was no cure for him. I have always found situations like this, which are unfortunately quite commonplace, some of the most difficult to deal with. People put their sincere faith in doctors, they trust us with their dearest possession of all, their lives, and when we run out of options, so invariably do they. Without doubt medicine has brought me some of the most immensely rewarding moments of my life, yet there have also been times when I have felt helpless, and this was one of them.

I often think to myself, *What would I do if I had reached that point in my life? Where would I go? How would I deal with my thoughts?* I know some people would argue that we all have only a limited amount of time to live, and I too am aware that after birth the only certain thing in life is death. And yet we actually know very little about what we are likely to experience at the end of life.

John was discharged the following day and I don't know what happened to him, as I moved away from that part of the hospital a few months later. However his memory stayed with me. I was also left wondering what we as a profession could offer someone if they wanted to know more about what they were likely to experience at the end of life. At the very least we should have an objective science that tells us what happens to us all when we die.

I think that NDEs hold the key to finally solving this mystery. In studying them further we will be able to discover the true nature of the relationship between the mind and the brain and answer the wider questions regarding the existence of an afterlife. Then we can live our lives with the knowledge of what fate will bring to us all.

Further information

If you would like more information or would like to support our research into the dying process, please visit the Horizon website: www.horizon-reserch.co.uk.

Here I have also listed a number of useful internet links that relate to the subjects discussed in this book.

The Horizon Research Foundation (*www.horizon-research.co.uk*). This is the website relating to the charitable foundation that we recently set up. It has general information on NDEs as well as on mind, brain and consciousness and further research. It is designed to be a resource centre for those interested in the science of what happens at the end of life.

The International Association for Near Death Studies (*www.iands.org*). The International Association of Near Death Studies is the first and largest organization on NDEs and this website is a very useful resource.

The Resuscitation Council (*www.resus.org.uk*). The UK Resuscitation Council's website provides general information on resuscitation issues.

The Nour Foundation (*www.nourfoundation.com* and *www.ostadelahi.com*). This is a very good website for links to the work of Professor Bahram Elahi. The Nour Foundation also explores the common moral, ethical and cultural principles underlying various philosophies and schools of thought through a host of multidisciplinary events by experts from such diverse fields as law, medicine, science, music and the arts. The philosophy of Ostad Elahi can also be accessed specifically on: *www.ostadelahi*.com.

The Center for Consciousness Studies (*www.consciousness.arizona.edu*). This is the website for the Center for Consciousness Studies at the University of Arizona and is a very good resource for consciousness studies. There are online courses and also conference details.

Stuart Hameroff (*www.quantumconsciousness.org*). This is Stuart Hameroff's website, where he explains his theories on consciousness being a quantum process. It is a very good website.

Particle Physics (*www.particleadventure.com*). This award-winning website explains particle physics to non-specialists and lay people wonderfully.

Recommended Reading

Although there follows a very complete bibliography regarding the main issues in this book, for many people a short recommended reading list may be more helpful. Therefore the following are selected reading materials from the bibliography.

Chapter 1: Near Death Experiences from Antiquity to the Present Day

Blackmore, S. J., 'Near death experiences', *Journal of the Royal Society of Medicine* 89 (1996), 73–6

Fenwick, P., and Fenwick, E., *The Truth in the Light*, Hodder Headline, 1995

Jansen, K., 'Near death experience and the NMDA receptor', *BMJ* 298 (1989), 1708

Moody, R. A., *Life After Life*, Bantam Press, 1975

Roberts, G., and Owen, J., 'The near-death experience', *British Journal of Psychiatry* 153 (Nov. 1988), 607–17

Chapter 4: The Scientific Paradox

Paradis, N. A., Halperin, H. A., and Nowak, R. A., *Cardiac Arrest: The Science and Practice of Resuscitation Medicine*, Williams and Wilkins, 1996

Parnia, S., and Fenwick, P., 'Near death experiences in cardiac arrest: visions of a dying brain or visions of a new science of consciousness', *Resuscitation* 52 (Jan. 2002), 1, 5–11

Chapter 5: Understanding Mind, Brain and Consciousness

Blackmore, S., *Consciousness: An Introduction*, Hodder and Stoughton, 2003

Chalmers, D. J., 'The puzzle of conscious experience', 'Mysteries of the Mind', *Scientific American* (special issue), 1997, 30–37

Crick, F., and Koch, C., 'The problem of consciousness', 'Mysteries of the Mind', *Scientific American* (special issue), 1997

Eccles, J. C., and Popper, K., *The Self and its Brain*, Routledge, 2003

Editorial, 'Mysteries of the Mind', *Scientific American* (special issue), 1997

Elahi, B., *Foundations of Natural Spirituality: A scientific approach to the nature of the spiritual self*, Element Books, 1998

—, *Spirituality is a Science*, Cornwall Books, 1999

—, *Medicine of the Soul*, Cornwall Books, 2001

Penrose, R., *Shadows of the Mind*, Oxford University Press, 1994

Chapter 6: The Ingredients of Life

Gribbin, J., *Almost Everyone's Guide to Science*, Yale University Press, 2000

Chapter 7: Is It Real?

Henslin, J., *Down to Earth Sociology: Introductory readings*, 13th edition, Free Press, 2005

Newberg, A., *Why God Won't Go Away: Brain science and the biology of belief*, Ballantine Books, 2002

Bibliography

Chapter 1: Near Death Experiences from Antiquity to the Present Day

Appleton, R. E., 'Reflex anoxic seizures', *British Medical Journal* 307 (1993), 214–15

Blackmore, S. J., 'Near death experiences', *Journal of the Royal Society of Medicine* 89 (1996), 73–6

Blackmore, S. J., and Troscianko, T., 'The physiology of the tunnel', *Journal for Near Death Studies* 8 (1988), 15–28

Carr, D., 'Pathophysiology of stress-induced limbic lobe dysfunction: a hypothesis for NDEs', *J. Near Death Studies* 2 (1982), 75–89

Carr, D. B., 'Endorphins at the approach of death', *Lancet* (1981), 1/8216, 390

Feng, Z., 'A research on near death experiences of survivors in big earthquake of Tangshan, 1976', *Chung Hua Shen Ching Ching Shen KO Tsa Chih* 25 (Aug. 1992), 222–5, 253–4

Fenwick, P., and Fenwick, E., *The Truth in the Light*, Hodder Headline, 1995

Gallup, G., *Adventures in Immortality: A look beyond the threshold of death*, McGraw-Hill, 1982

Greyson, B., 'Near-death experiences and attempted suicide', *Suicide Life Threatening Behaviour* 11 (Spring 1981), 1, 10–16

—, 'Near death experiences and personal values', *American Journal of Psychiatry* 140 (May 1983), 5, 618–20

—, 'The near death experience scale construction, reliability, and validity', *Journal of Nervous Mental Disease* 171 (1983), 369–75

—, 'Incidence of NDEs following attempted suicide', *Suicide Life Threat. Behav.* 16 (Spring 1986), 1, 40–5

—, 'The near-death experience as a focus of clinical attention', *J. Nerv. Ment. Dis.* 185 (May 1997), 5, 327–34

—, 'Dissociation in people who have near-death experiences: out of their bodies or out of their minds?', *Lancet* 355, 5 February 2000, 9202, 460–3

Heim, A., 'Notizen über den Tod durch Absturz', *Jahrbuch des schweizer. Alpenclub* 27 (1892), 327–37

Herzog, D. B., and Herrin, J. T., 'Near-death experiences in the very young', *Critical Care Medicine* 13 (Dec. 1985), 12, 1074–5

Jansen, K., 'Near death experience and the NMDA receptor', *BMJ* 298 (1989), 1708

Kellehear, A., 'Culture, biology, and the near death experience', *J. Nerv. Ment. Dis.* 181 (1993), 148–56

Kelly, E. W., 'Near-death experiences with reports of meeting deceased people', *Death Stud.* 25 (Apr.–May 2001), 3, 229–49

Lempert, T., 'Syncope and near death experience', *Lancet* 344 (1994), 829–30

Meduna, L., *Carbon Dioxide Therapy: A neurophysiological treatment of nervous disorders*, 2nd edition, Charles C. Thomas Publisher, 1958

Moody, R. A., *Life after Life*, Bantam Press, 1975

Morse, M. L., 'Near death experiences of children', *J. Ped. Onc. Nursing* 11 (1994), 139–44

Morse, M., Castillo, P., Venecia, D., Milstein, J., and Tyler, D. C., 'Childhood near death experiences', *Am. J. Dis. Child* 140 (1986), 1110–14

Morse, M., Venecia, D., and Milstein, J., 'Near-death experiences: A neurophysiologic explanatory model', *J. Near Death Studies* 8 (1989), 1, 45–53

Noyes, R., and Kletti, R., 'Depersonalisation in the face of life threatening danger: a description', *Psychiatry* 39 (1976), 251–9

Osis, K., and Haraldsson, E., *At the Hour of Death*, Avon Books, 1977

Owens, J. E., Cook, E. W., and Stevenson, I., 'Features of "near death experience" in relation to whether or not patients were near death', *Lancet* 336 (1990), 1175–7

Pascricha, S., and Stevenson, I., 'Near death experiences in India', *J. Nerv. Ment. Dis.* 55 (Oct. 1986), 4, 542–9

Plato, *The Republic*, J. M. Dent & Sons, 1937

Ring, K., *Life at Death: A scientific investigation of the near-death experience*, Coward McCann and Geoghenan, 1980

Roberts, G., and Owen, J., 'The near-death experience', *Br. J. Psychiatry* 153 (Nov. 1988), 607–17

Serdahely, W. J., 'Pediatric near death experiences', *Journal of Near Death Studies* 9 (1990), 1

Sotelo, J., Perez, R., Guevara, P., and Fernandez, A., 'Changes in brain, plasma and cerebrospinal fluid contents of B-endorphin in dogs at the moment of death', *Neurological Research* 17 (June 1995), 223

Whinnery, J. E., and Whinnery, A. M., 'Acceleration-induced loss of consciousness', *Arch. Neurol.* 47 (1990), 764–76

Chapter 4: The Scientific Paradox

(a) Near Death Experiences in Cardiac Arrest

Greyson, B., 'Incidence and correlates of near-death experiences in a cardiac care unit', *General Hospital Psychiatry* 25 (July–Aug. 2003), 4, 269–76

Martens, P. R., 'Near-death-experiences in out-of-hospital cardiac arrest survivors: meaningful phenomena or just fantasy of death?', *Resuscitation* 27 (Mar. 1994), 2, 171–5

Parnia, S., Waller, D., Yeates, R., and Fenwick, P., 'A qualitative and quantitative study of the incidence, features and aetiology of near death experiences in cardiac arrest survivors', *Resuscitation* 48 (Feb. 2001), 149–56

Parnia, S., and Fenwick, P., 'Near death experiences in cardiac arrest: visions of a dying brain or visions of a new science of consciousness?', *Resuscitation* 52 (Jan. 2002) 1, 5–11

Ring, K., *Life at Death: A scientific investigation of the near-death experience*, Coward McCann and Geoghenan, 1980

Schwaninger, J., 'A prospective analysis of near death experiences in cardiac arrest patients', *Journal of Near Death Experiences* 20 (2002), 4

Van Lommel, P., Van Wees, R., Meyers, V., and Elfferich, I., 'Near-death experience in survivors of cardiac arrest: a prospective study in the Netherlands', *Lancet*, 358, 15 Dec. 2001, (9298), 2039–45

(b) Brain Blood Flow and Physiology during Cardiac Arrest

Angelos, M., Safar, P., Reich, H., 'A comparison of cardiopulmonary resuscitation with cardiopulmonary bypass after prolonged cardiac arrest in dogs: reperfusion pressures and neurologic recovery', *Resuscitation* 21 (1991), 121–35

Buunk, G., Van der Hoeven, J. G., and Meinders, A. E., 'Cerebral blood flow after cardiac arrest', *The Netherlands Journal of Medicine* 57 (2000), 106–12

Cartlidge, N., 'Head injury, outcome and prognosis' in M. Swash and J. Oxbury (eds), *Clinical Neurology*, vol. I, Churchill Livingstone, 1991

Cerchiari, E. L., Hoel, T. M., Safar, P., and Sclabassi, R. J., 'Protective effects of combined superoxide dismutase and deferoxamine on recovery of cerebral blood flow and function after cardiac arrest in dogs', *Stroke* 18 (1987), 869–78

Clute, H. L., and Levy, W. J., 'Electroencephalographic changes during brief cardiac arrest in humans', *Anesthesiology* 73 (1990), 821–5

De Vries, J. *et al.*, 'Changes in cerebral oxygen uptake and cerebral electrical activity during defibrillation threshold testing', *Anesth. Analg.* 87 (1998), 16–20

Drejer, J., Benveniste, H., Diemer, N. Y. *et al.*, 'Cellular origin of ischemic-induced glutamate release from brain tissue in vivo and in vitro', *J. Neurochem* 45 (1985), 145–50

Fischer, M., and Hossman, K. A., 'Volume expansion during cardiopulmonary resuscitation reduces cerebral no-reflow', *Resuscitation* 32 (1996), 227–40

Gonzalez, E. R., Ornato, J. P., and Garnett, A. R., 'Dose dependent vasopressor response to epinephrine during CPR in human beings', *Ann. Emerg. Med.* 18 (1991), 920–6

Kano, T., Hashiguchi, A., and Sadanaga, M., 'Cardiopulmonary-cerebral resuscitation by using cardiopulmonary bypass through the femoral vein and artery in dogs', *Resuscitation* 25 (1993), 265–81

Krause, G. S., White, B. C., Aust, S. D., Nayini, N. R., and Kumar, K., 'Brain cell death following ischemia and reperfusion: a proposed biochemical sequence', *Crit. Care Med.* 16 (1988), 714–26

Lavy, S., and Stern, S., 'Electroencephalographic changes following sudden cessation of artificial pacing in patients with heart block', *Confin. Neurol.* 29 (1967) (Basel), 47

Lishman, W. A., 'Head Injury' in *Organic Psychiatry*, 2nd edition, Blackwells, 1987

Longstaff, A., *Instant Notes in Neuroscience*, BIOS Scientific Publishers, 2000

Marshall, R. S., Lazar, R. M., and Spellman, J. P., 'Recovery of brain function during induced cerebral hypoperfusion' *Brain* 124 (2001), 1208–17

Mayer, J., and Marx, T., 'The Pathogenesis of EEG Changes during Cerebral Anoxia' in J. Van Der Drift (ed.), *Cardiac and Vascular Diseases Handbook of Electro-encephalography and Clinicial Neurophysiology*, Amsterdam, 1972

Paradis, N. A., Martin, G. B., and Goetting, M. G., 'Simultaneous aortic jugular bulb, and right atrial pressures during cardiopulmonary resuscitation in humans: insights into mechanisms', *Circulation* 80 (1989), 361–8

Paradis, N. A., Martin, G. B., and Rosenberg, J., 'The effect of standard and high dose epinephrine on coronary perfusion pressure during prolonged cardiopulmonary resuscitation', *Journal of the American Medical Association* 265 (1991), 1139–44

Paradis, N. A., Halperin, H. A., and Nowak, R. A., *Cardiac Arrest: The science and practice of resuscitation medicine*, Williams and Wilkins, 1996

Teasdale, G., 'Head Injury: Concussion, coma and recovery from altered states of consciousness' in M. Swash and J. Oxbury (eds), *Clinical Neurology*, Churchill Livingstone, 1991

Traynelis, S. F., and Cull-Candy, S. G., 'Proton inhibition of N-methyl-D-Aspartate receptors in cerebellar neurons', *Nature* 345 (1990), 347–50

Chapter 5: Understanding Mind, Brain and Consciousness

Beck, F., and Eccles, J. C., 'Quantum aspects of brain activity and the role of consciousness', *Proceedings of the National Academy of Science USA* 89 (1 Dec. 1992), 23, 11357–61

Blackmore, S., *Consciousness: An Introduction*, Hodder and Stoughton, 2003

Britton, W. B., and Bootzin, R. R., 'Near-death experiences and the temporal lobe', *Psychol Sci.* 15 (Apr. 2004), 4, 254–8

Chalmers, D. J., 'The puzzle of conscious experience', 'Mysteries of the Mind', *Scientific American* (special issue), 1997, 30–37

—, *The Conscious Mind: In search of a fundamental theory*, Oxford University Press, 1997

Crick, F., and Koch, C., 'Consciousness and neuroscience', *Cerebral Cortex* 8 (Mar. 1998), 2, 97–107

Dennett, D., 'Are we explaining consciousness yet?', *Cognition* 79 (Apr. 2001), 1–2, 221–37

—, *Consciousness Explained*, Back Bay Books, 1992

'Does neuroscience threaten human values?' *Nature Neuroscience*, Nov. 1998, 1, 535–6

Eccles, J. C., Evolution of consciousness', *Proc. Natl. Acad. Sci. USA* 89 (15 Aug. 1992), 16, 7320–4

—, *Evolution of the Brain: Creation of the self*, Routledge, 2001

Eccles, J. C., and Popper, K., *The Self and its Brain*, Routledge 2003

Editorial, 'Mysteries of the Mind', *Scientific American* (special issue), 1997

Elahi, B., *Foundations of Natural Spirituality: A scientific approach to the nature of the spiritual self*, Element Books, 1998

—, *Spirituality is a Science*, Cornwall Books, 1999

—, *Medicine of the Soul*, Cornwall Books, 2001

Fenwick, P., 'Current Methods of Investigation in Neuroscience' in M. Velmans (ed.), *Investigating Phenomenal Consciousness*, John Benjamins Publishing Company, 2000

Flohr, H., 'An information processing theory of anaesthesia', *Neuropsychologia* 33 (Sept. 1995), 9, 1169–80

Flohr, H., Glade, U., and Motzko, D., 'The role of the NMDA synapse in general anesthesia', *Toxicol. Lett.*, 23 Nov. 1998, 100–101, 23–9

Frackowiak, R., Friston, K., Frith, C., Dolan, R., and Mazziotta, J. C., *Human Brain Function*, Academic Press, 1997

Freeman, W., 'Consciousness, intentionality and causality', *Journal of Consciousness Studies* 6 (1999), 11–12, 143–72

French, C. C., 'Dying to know the truth: visions of a dying brain, or false memories?', *Lancet* 358, 15 December 2001, 9298, 2010–1

Greenfield, S, 'Mind, brain and consciousness', *British Journal of Psychiatry* 181 (Aug. 2002), 91–3

Hameroff, S., Nip, A., Porter, M., and Tuszynski, J., 'Conduction pathways in microtubules, biological quantum computation, and consciousness', *Biosystems* 64 (Jan. 2002), 1–3, 149–68

Huettel, S. A., Song, A. W., and McCarthy, G., *Functional Magnetic Resonance Imaging*, book and CD-Rom edition, Sinauer Associates, 2004

Kandel, E. R., Schwartz, J. H., and Jessell, T., *Principles of Neural Science*, MacGraw-Hill, 2000

Penrose, R., *Shadows of the Mind*, Oxford University Press, 1994

—, 'Consciousness, the brain, and spacetime geometry: an addendum. Some new developments on the Orch OR model for consciousness', *Ann. NY Acad. Sci.* 929, (Apr. 2001), 105–10

Ramachandran, R., *A Brief Tour of Human Consciousness: From impostor poodles to purple numbers*, Pi Press, 2004

Rees, G., Kreiman, G., and Koch, C., 'Neural correlates of consciousness in humans', *Nat. Rev. Neurosci.* 3 (Apr. 2002), 4, 261–70

Searle, J., 'The mystery of consciousness', *New York Review of Books*, 1997

—, 'Do we understand consciousness?', *Journal of Consciousness Studies* 5 (1998), 5–6, 718–33

Tononi, G., and Edelman, G. M., 'Consciousness and complexity', *Science* 282 (4 Dec. 1998), 5395, 1846–51

Valk, P. E., Bailey, D. L., Townsend, D. W., and Maisey, M. N., *Positron Emission Tomography: Basic science and clinical practice*, Springer, 2003

Chapter 6: The Ingredients of Life

Asimov, I., and Bach, D. F., *Atom: Journey across the Subatomic Cosmos*, Plume Books, 1992

Gribbin, J., *Almost Everyone's Guide to Science*, Yale University Press, 2000

Griffiths, D., *Introduction to Elementary Particles*, John Wiley & Sons, 1987

Kuhn, K. F., *Basic Physics: A self-teaching guide*, 2nd edition, John Wiley & Sons, 1996

Martin, B. R., and Shaw, G., *Particle Physics*, 2nd edition, John Wiley & Sons, 1997

Chapter 7: Is It Real?

Blanke, O., 'Out of body experiences and their neural basis', *BMJ* 329, 18 December 2004, 7480, 1414–15

Blanke, O., Ortigue, S., Landis, T., and Seeck, M., 'Stimulating illusory own-body perceptions', *Nature* 419, 19 September 2002, 6904, 269–70

Blanke, O., and Arzy, S., 'The out-of-body experience: disturbed self-processing at the temporo-parietal junction', *Neuroscientist* 11 (Feb. 2005), 1, 16–24

Henslin, J., *Down to Earth Sociology: Introductory Readings*, 13th edition, Free Press, 2005

Newberg, A., *Why God Won't Go Away: Brain science and the biology of belief*, Ballantine Books, 2002

Newberg, A. B., and Iversen, J., 'The neural basis of the complex mental task of meditation: neurotransmitter and neurochemical considerations', *Medical Hypotheses* 61 (Aug. 2003), 2, 282–91

Newberg, A., Pourdehnad, M., Alavi, A., and d'Aquili, E. G., 'Cerebral blood flow during meditative prayer: preliminary findings and methodological issues', *Percept. Mot. Skills* 97 (Oct. 2003), 2, 625–30

Penfield, W., *The Excitable Cortex in Conscious Man*, Liverpool University Press, 1958

Chapter 9: Implications for the Future

The references quoted in this chapter have all been included in chapters 4–7.

Index

Page numbers for illustrations are given in *italics*; main references are given in **bold**. References to the text accompanying an illustration are given in normal type. References for NDE features are general; main features (e.g. lights and tunnels) have their own main headings.

We hope you enjoyed this Hay House book.
If you would like to receive a free catalogue featuring additional
Hay House books and products, or if you would like information
about the Hay Foundation, please contact:

Hay House UK Ltd
Unit 62, Canalot Studios • 222 Kensal Rd • London W10 5BN
Tel: (44) 20 8962 1230; Fax: (44) 20 8962 1239
www.hayhouse.co.uk
****

Published and distributed in the United States of America by:
Hay House, Inc. • P.O. Box 5100 • Carlsbad, CA 92018-5100
Tel: (1) 760 431 7695 or (800) 654 5126; Fax: (1) 760 431 6948 or (800) 650 5115
www.hayhouse.com
****

Published and distributed in Australia by:
Hay House Australia Ltd • 18/36 Ralph St • Alexandria NSW 2015
Tel: (61) 2 9669 4299 • Fax: (61) 2 9669 4144
www.hayhouse.com.au
****

Published and distributed in the Republic of South Africa by:
Hay House SA (Pty) Ltd • PO Box 990 • Witkoppen 2068
Tel/Fax: (27) 11 706 6612 • orders@psdprom.co.za
****

Distributed in Canada by:
Raincoast • 9050 Shaughnessy St • Vancouver, BC V6P 6E5
Tel: (1) 604 323 7100 • Fax: (1) 604 323 2600
****

Sign up via the Hay House UK website to receive the Hay House
online newsletter and stay informed about what's going on with
your favourite authors. You'll receive bimonthly announcements
about discounts and offers, special events, product highlights,
free excerpts, giveaways, and more!

www.hayhouse.co.uk